He Don't Look Like Elvis

Frank C. Siraguso

For Bob, Barry, Charles, Rufus, Hollywood Bob, and Bobby Love, who put it all together.

And for Anne, who put me on the Hot List.

He Don't Look Like Elvis

Write the Future
1800 W. 39th Street
Kansas City, Missouri 64111

Copyright © 2017
Frank C. Siraguso

First Print Edition
1 3 5 7 9 10 8 6 4 2

ISBN: 978-0-9983843-3-7
Library of Congress Control Number: 2017917334

Printed in the United States of America

Cover and Layout
Macattack Design

Photographs of Bobby Love on stage, copyright © 2017 Frank C. Siraguso

All rights reserved. No part of this publication may be reproduced or transmitted in any form or by any means, electronic or mechanical, including photocopying, recording or information retrieval system, without prior written permission from the publisher.

Acknowledgments

I offer my heartfelt thanks and gratitude to the poets, writers and special people, all of whom are my dear friends, who helped me with editing, proofing, mentoring, reading, and just figuring out how to write.

To wit: David Ray; Debra Di Blasi; Julie Mierau; Mariah Andrews (who took a chance); Nina Gibson; Rosemary O'Leary, PhD; and my wonderful wife, Molly O'Leary, DC.

CONTENTS

An Urgent Message 11
Atchison 53
Minot 69
Chillicothe 99
Photos 126
Glasgow 131
Where The Hell Is Poplar Bluff? 145
Monroe Inn Redux 169
Bobby Love World Tour 175
Final Curtain 199

He Don't Look Like Elvis

It's gotta be true. Nobody could make this shit up.
— Barry Johnson

An Urgent Message

"I have some interesting news."

Anne, my wife, had walked upstairs and was standing in the bathroom doorway. I was at the sink, shaving, getting ready to shower off the dust and warm up at the end of a cold, hard winter's day. My job as a land surveyor for the city of Kansas City, Missouri, kept me outside all day, every day.

"Oh yeah?" I looked askance at her, trying to shave without drawing blood.

"Some guy named Bobby Love called and said he needed a bass player for his show. He does a lot of fifties and sixties, oldies."

"How'd he get my name?"

"About a week ago I called the Musicians' union and put your name on the Hot List."

She did? This was the first I'd heard of it.

"When did he call?"

"Not long before you got home. He said he would call back."

Well, this was interesting news.

As far as I was concerned, I was through with bands and music. Although I hadn't really quit Foxfire, the band I had been with for the last three years, about a month earlier we had descended into Limbo. Foxfire included the Cobb brothers Cliff, Danny and Sam. They were good players with killer vocals. We had been friends since high school and enjoyed playing music together. But the combination of too much rehearsal and too few gigs did us in.

The ignominious end came when we played a dance for Northeast High School at some hall they rented. That night it was five below zero and snowing like hell. Even so, we managed not to drop anything or fall on our asses while moving equipment from our cars to the stage. We got the amps, drums and PA set up and ready to go in good time. We turned it all on, tuned up, and did a sound check.

The PA wasn't working. We had no microphones. It took us most of a frantic hour to get that ironed out, and by then the crowd was damn near murderous. When we finally did start playing, the crowd liked us OK but the mood was broken. At the end of the night, one of the adults demanded that we "pro-rate our fee," as he put it. So not only was it a crappy gig, we made less money.

That was the last straw. Suffering a lot of frustration, we had decided unanimously, by osmosis, without even bothering to discuss it, to take a long break. It was the unspoken thing.

Foxfire was an artistic success but a commercial failure. That miserable Northeast gig was the icing on the cake. That was it for me. Foxfire would be the last in my series of attempts to become a rich and famous rock star. I was ready to relax and succumb to the workaday life. Being a surveyor was kind of a neat job with a sense of history to it. There were the Egyptians and the pyramids, the Romans and the aqueducts, and Lewis and Clark, explorers and mapmakers. Once I got used to being out in extremes of heat and cold – especially the cold! – it was easy. All I had to do was show up in the morning and go to work. No endless rehearsals, no lugging band equipment at all hours, no working two jobs, only one of which really paid. Hell, I could have gone back to school and finished a degree, and the City would have paid for it!

An Urgent Message

I was ready to bow out.

And then, just as I was getting comfortable with the idea but before I could think to discuss it with Anne, I'm on the Hot List and some guy named Bobby Love wants to talk to me. I had a dizzy, here-I-go-again feeling.

Right on cue, just after my shower, the phone rang.

Hesitating, I gave it a couple of beats, then answered. A smoky, raspy barroom voice was on the line.

"This is Bobby Love."

After the basic formalities, I asked him what kind of stuff he did.

"Oh, fifties, sixties, oldies stuff. And I do an Elvis tribute."

An Elvis tribute.

Elvis Presley died August 16, 1977. It was a Tuesday. I was on my way home from work, sweltering in my car on Southwest Trafficway, when I heard the news on NPR. Janis and Jimi, I could believe. But who could think that Elvis would become another rock 'n' roll fatality?

The King was dead, and into the vacuum rushed a new genre of performer: the Elvis impersonator or, as some said, Elvis imitator. Every band does cover renditions of their favorite songs, even the early Beatles did it. But to assume someone's personality seemed, well, weird and distasteful at best. It would never occur to any musician I knew. Maybe there were always impersonators, but until after Elvis died I had never heard of such a thing. Yet, all of a sudden, Elvis impersonators were cropping up everywhere, thicker than fleas on a hound dog. And now, with the King barely six months gone, I was confronted with the prospect of working with one.

What the hell. It sounded interesting. Contrary to my feelings about another band, I arranged to meet him at the Monroe Inn the coming Saturday afternoon. That gave me four days to stew in it.

My vision of the scenario was this: I'd go down there and jam around a little, find it unproductive, then come home and forget about it.

Saturday came and I was still stewing. For moral support and to get a second opinion, I had asked JB, a friend who also knew the Cobbs, to lend me the use of his person and VW bus to haul my amp, bass and ass to meet Bobby Love. He arrived about twelve thirty, and we loaded up and took off.

JB fired up a joint. "So you got an audition today, huh? What happened with you and Foxfire? Did the Cobb brothers flip out or what?"

"Fuck. I think it was that last gig that Morris got us. It would have been OK if the PA hadn't crapped out. It was cold, what, five below? Snow, all that shit. And then the PA wouldn't work. Boy, that was the worst moment of my life. After that, nothing bothers me. And besides, those other guys weirded out, thinking that Morris was trying to gyp 'em or something. After he helped them buy their amps! Maybe he wasn't the best manager, but he wasn't a crook. On top of that, they never felt ready to work. We'd still be rehearsing. So, hell. Anne turned my name in to the union, and this Bobby Love guy calls and says he needs a bass player."

"Oh yeah? What kind of stuff does he do?"

"He says it's fifties and oldies, some Elvis stuff. A tribute or something. It could be weird, especially being at the Monroe Inn."

"Did he say anything about going on the road? I bet it would be nice to be out of town for a while."

"Aw, I don't know. He said something about maybe going on the road, but I don't know. I don't really want to travel. Anne would have to keep working, and I'd be gone. That'd be a drag. It'd be nice if they'd work in town, but I don't know. There's not that much stuff going on here." I took a hit off the joint. "Boy, this is sure gonna be bizarre. Do you know where to go?"

"No. It's somewhere on Independence Avenue, right?"

"Yeah, Independence and Monroe. Get off the freeway at Truman Road."

The Monroe Inn was over in Northeast, the Kansas City neighborhood where I grew up. I knew just where it was. Northeast is decidedly working class and ethnic, in those days mostly Italians and various Europeans. It was starting to run down from urban neglect, but the inhabitants were still proud.

"So," goaded JB, "you don't want to go on the road, huh? Look, you've been doing this for years. This could be your chance to be in a band that works instead of practices all the time. What do you want, to be stuck all your life?"

"I've got to check it out, you're right. Man, this has got to be bizarre."

We pulled up on the south side of the avenue, across from the Monroe Inn. JB made a hairy U-turn and it was curb service.

We sat and looked the place over for a minute. I was having second thoughts.

Although it was mid-February, it had warmed up to about forty-five degrees, sort of a midwinter break. The sky was cloudy, wind chilly, the air was clean and crisp, and the sidewalks still damp from a morning rain.

"Boy, it'd be real easy to leave and just forget it. This seems pretty weird to me. But this is the place, all right."

"Aw, man, it's karma. Get out and go see."

Karma. Yeah.

The Monroe Inn sat on the northeast corner of Independence Avenue and Monroe, facing the avenue. Next to it was a Mexican restaurant, essentially an extension of the same building but with a different facade and separate entrance. I was looking for a side door, something that would be less obtrusive than taking my equipment through the front door of the tavern. The Monroe Inn's entrance was on the corner, but there was a door with no window next to the restaurant entrance. I pulled the handle. Locked. But just then a man opened it and came out.

He wore jeans, a polyester shirt and black leather sport coat. He had black curly hair, steel-grey eyes, and a complexion like the Pillsbury Doughboy. He was shorter than me, but wiry, about five ten. We looked at each other.

"You must be Bobby Love," I said, as if I had always known.

"That's right, heh-heh. Are you Frank?" There was that same barroom voice.

"Yeah." We shook hands.

"Well, come on in and we'll get started. The drummer and guitar player won't be here today, but the arranger is."

The side door opened to a large dance floor with a bandstand up against the wall shared with the restaurant. It looked just like any other bar in the daytime. Empty and dark.

This was the largest room in the joint. A large archway across from the bandstand led to the long, narrow barroom, where a few regulars sat quietly drinking and talking. The bandstand stood about four feet off the floor, with a wooden rail around it that made it look like a cattle pen. No lights were on, except one shining on the stage. A guy was up there listening to a tape. He appeared to be his middle twenties, about five eight, slight build, with well groomed, long brown hair and a short beard.

"Frank," said Bobby, "this is Bob Buster, our trumpet player and arranger." We shook hands.

"Well," began Bob, businesslike, "we got a tape of some songs here that we do for the dance set. Why don't I play it and see what you think, OK?"

"Sure. Let me get my bass and amp." JB helped me bring in the amp and set it up on the stage. Then he went to the bar for a beer and retired to a table in a dark corner at the back of the room. When I was ready, Bob put a tape in the player.

"If you know some of them, fine. And the rest, see if you think you could learn 'em."

"While you guys do that," said Bobby, moving toward the bar, "I'm gonna get a beer."

Bob miked the cassette player through the band's PA system so I could hear it better. I recognized the songs and knew how to play some of them. Still, I followed along on the bass well enough to fool non-musicians into believing I had actually practiced this stuff. Bob listened approvingly. By this time, Bobby had wandered back and was standing on the dance floor, next to the stage. Bob and I were sitting up on the rail.

"Sounds good!" Bobby was pleased. "Fretless bass, huh?"

My interest in music started early. When I was about four or five years old, around 1955, my dad ran a bar in Kansas City, the 3929 Club. The house band was a country-western outfit led by Clayton Howerton, a guitar player. Clayton could make that guitar talk and the ladies swoon.

Sometimes my mom and her friends would go to the 3929 Club to hang out, and sometimes they'd take me. I liked to watch the band. They dressed in white western shirts with green saguaro cactuses on the front and pearl snaps for buttons. They wore white, low-crowned Stetson cowboy hats. Clayton played a Gibson, but the other guitar player had one of the new Fender Stratocaster guitars. I have always thought the country players liked Stratocasters because their shape resembled the saguaro.

Lynn Estes, the bass player, played an upright bass. For some reason, I liked to get up on the stage and mess with the bass. Lynn would let me pluck the strings for a few minutes and would even put his Stetson on my head. I can still see that bright-crimson satin lining.

I began learning to play guitar around 1957, inspired by Elvis. In first grade, Sister Joseph Benedict told us "Elvis is a worker of the Devil." We were not convinced. "No, he's not," said my cousin Joanne. By 1962 I was learning Ventures tunes and after the Beatles hit, my fate was sealed. From then on, I was determined to be a musician and play in a band.

Soon after the British Invasion I started playing bass. I was pretty good as a guitar player and played rhythm and some lead in bands during high school. But guitar players were plentiful and bass players scarce. Besides, I had an affinity for the bass and nobody else could play it as well. I couldn't afford a Fender or Gibson, but found a cool violin-shaped bass, a la Paul McCartney, in the Spiegel catalog for seventy-nine dollars. For a relatively cheap bass, it was pretty nice. By the time I was ready to start college, in 1969, I had retired from bands and had sold all my band gear except for my Gibson Blue Ridge acoustic guitar.

Retirement was short-lived. In 1972, I actually quit college to make a serious go at being a musician in a band with my old high school friends. This time it was more than temporary insanity.

To earn money to buy a bass and amp, I took a job with the City of Kansas City as a land surveyor. We staked out roads, sidewalks and sewer lines for construction, and performed different types of surveys such as property surveys to determine if a property was on city land, and legal surveys to help determine whether the city or property owner was liable for say, damage caused by a fallen tree. We also did preliminary surveys to determine where city buildings or roads might go. I figured to be there six months or so, while I got new equipment and the band got going. It would be a long six months.

An Urgent Message

I bought a new Sunn amp and a Fender Precision bass. These were the days when guitar amplifiers were reaching ever more gigantic proportions. Everyone had amp envy. Guitar players took their cues from Eric Clapton in Cream. On stage, Clapton was dwarfed by his tower of Marshall amp speakers, the infamous Marshall stack, blasting louder than a fighter jet. Guys dreamed of amps as big as a house, with a kill radius of two miles. Never mind how to carry them or get them in and out of small bars. The Beatles had started it with their Vox amps, those neat black boxes with the trapezoid power heads, the diamond-patterned grille cloth and cool sound.

The Who used Sunn amps. What really sold me on Sunn, though, was seeing a local band, the Burlington Express, at the Place, a psychedelic club in Westport, while still in high school. The bass player had a stack of Sunn speakers that reached to the ceiling. Their clear sound pinned us to the back wall. Sunn didn't have all the bells and whistles of Vox amps, but they were solid, dependable, and had a great tone.

I got a Coliseum 880 that had four 15-inch speakers, two each in two dresser-sized cabinets. The power head weighed about 25 pounds and pushed 320 watts. I loved it. In all the time I used that amp, I never had to turn the volume up past 4 (out of 10).

My bass was one of Fender's new fretless models. Leo Fender introduced his solid-body Precision bass, the first electric bass, in 1951. He had already put his stamp on music history in 1948 with the Broadcaster, soon renamed the Telecaster. Easy to manufacture, the Tele was one of the first practical, solid-body electric guitars. (Fender competed neck and neck, as it were, with Les Paul and Gibson.)

Fender's electric bass guitar was a hybrid. It combined the low notes of the bass violin, also called in musician vernacular the upright bass, stand-up bass or doghouse bass, with the amplified sound and wieldy size of the solid-body electric guitar. While the upright bass still holds sway in jazz, by 1957 Fender's Precision bass was becoming favored over the upright in country-western and rockabilly bands.

This was the final piece of the puzzle. The smooth, smoky sound of the acoustic upright was replaced by the hard-edged, electric sound of the bass guitar. This, more than anything, gave the gut punch to what was becoming rock 'n' roll.

It wasn't long before most guitar companies included a bass in their line as well. For a while, the Paul McCartney's violin-shaped Hofner bass caused a stir. However, the Fender Precision, looking like a large Stratocaster, was the benchmark, the gold standard. If a bass player wanted to look like he knew what he was about, the Fender Precision or its snappier cousin, the Fender Jazz bass, was the hot setup.

By the time I bought my Precision, in 1973, electric basses had even crept into jazz use, especially in fusion jazz, a combination (some would call it a bastardization) of jazz and rock. But some jazz bassists missed the smooth feel and sound of the upright, so they filed the frets off their basses. Frets on a guitar neck allow proper intonation (hence, the Precision in Fender's name). Bass violins, as well as violins, violas and cellos, have no frets. Fender took the hint and began making fretless basses.

I had played upright in the college jazz band and I, too, liked the feel and the sound. The bass I ordered, sunburst finish with a rosewood neck, cost $307. Oddly enough, Fender's fretless basses were the least expensive (they saved money by not installing frets). When Jim, the salesman at Jack Need's Pro Shop, called to tell me it was in, I rushed down there pronto. Jim sheepishly informed me that they had accidentally sent a bass with a maple neck and that I owed him another $14. I might have argued the point but when I actually saw the instrument it looked so great I was speechless. I was glad they screwed up and I forked over the loot. As fate would have it, all I had on me was fourteen bucks. So, the Precision bass with maple neck cost $321, and I never fretted over it.

"Fretless bass, huh?" Bobby mused. "Pretty wild. I've always been afraid of fretless basses because most guys don't play 'em in tune. But I think you'll do all right."

"Yeah, he picked the stuff right up, Bobby," agreed Bob.

"What other kind of music do you do?" I asked Bobby. "You said something about fifties stuff, and some Elvis tunes?"

"Yeah, I do an Elvis tribute. I do his fifties songs and the Vegas act. I got costumes and a spotlight. A regular show. I give away scarves like Elvis did, and I'm gonna have some pictures of me in costume taken, and sell them as souvenirs."

"Well, I don't think I'd have any trouble." I was confident. "Some of the tunes I've never played before, but I could do the songs. Are you going on the road?"

"We'll probably have to sooner or later," hedged Bobby. "There are a lot of rooms that I play around the country. But we're not going for a while yet. Why don't you listen to some more of that music, and I'll go get another drink, heh-heh."

Bob and I went back to work. "Here, this is some of the Elvis show," he said, turning on a cassette. As I listened, I glanced for a clue over at JB, still sitting in a dark corner nursing a beer. He smiled and shrugged.

A few songs into the show tape, Bob and I picked up on some commotion up front at the bar. Some guy had come through the front door talking loudly. We heard him before we saw him, and everybody at the bar was looking his direction. Finally, he ambled into sight near the end of the bar. He was about Bob's height, but built like a barrel. He was dressed totally in black: black shoes, black nylon socks, black slacks, a black guinea-T, a black leather coat and a black stingy-brim hat. He had black hair. He had a black aura. He wandered around the bar, spoiling for a fight, bothering the customers.

"I'm Italy, fuck Sicily! Man, I'm Italy, fuck Sicily." He pointed to his chest. "I'm tellin' ya, fuck Sicily, I'm Italy! I'll fight anybody to prove it! C'mon! Dammit! Fuck Sicily, I'm Italy!"

As he moved into the dance room, he spotted us. He slowly walked toward the bandstand, singing his refrain. From the floor next to the bandstand, he stood silent, menacingly glaring up at us. Now, my dad's folks were from Sicily, but I wasn't about to discuss it with this gibroni. We ignored him as long as we dared, then finally stopped work long enough to look down at him.

"Fuck Sicily, I'm Italy!"

Bob and I looked at each other, then stared dumbly back at "Italy."

"Say," he bellowed, "do you guys know any Led Zeppelin? Play some Led Zeppelin!"

"Gee, man, I'm new here," I said. "We don't know any songs together. I know some Zeppelin myself, if you want." I began playing the intro bass line from "Dazed and Confused." This seemed to bemuse him somewhat.

"Nah . . . that's OK." He turned and ambled back toward the bar. "Fuck Sicily, I'm Italy!" Bob and I looked at each other again. We didn't know if the guy was drunk, stoned, speeding, or all of the above. But he was gone.

Bobby came back from the bar with his beer, having skirted around the other side of the room to avoid Italy.

"Hey," Bobby said to us, "I'll give you five dollars to go over there and tell that guy he's an asshole." We passed.

By this time, Italy had moved to the bar, hassling the bartender. From where we stood, it looked like a sure fight. But the bartender nixed it, leaning into the guys face and motioning to the door with his thumb. I couldn't hear what he said, but Italy turned and strolled out, in no hurry, singing the same tune.

An Urgent Message

"Fuck Sicily, I'm Italy!"

We all looked at each other. Over in the corner, JB mopped his brow. "Bobby, do you know that guy?" I asked.

"Fuck no!" he said.

"You're kidding! I thought you knew him! I guess it's because you both have the same kind of coat."

"What?" Bobby was incredulous. "Man, I don't know that guy! I've never seen him before!"

We all breathed a deep sigh of relief. "Well, look," I continued, getting back to business, "do you have any charts or something so I can learn the songs?"

"We'll give you a list of the show tunes, in order, and a tape of the show," said Bobby. "I've got a lot of Elvis records, too, so you can learn the right parts. The ones on the show tape aren't right. I mean, the guy played OK, but I want it like the record."

"Great. No problem. When is the rest of the band going to be here?"

"Monday at five thirty. Can you make it?" asked Bobby.

"Yeah, but it'll be close. I get off work at five."

"See ya then."

So, that was it. That's all Bobby said.

JB helped me pack up and we went home.

"I can't believe it," I marveled, as we drove off.

"That sure was a weird place, man. That guy in black was something else!" laughed JB. "I'm glad he didn't see me in the corner."

"It's an omen: This is going to be bizarre."

Anne laughed when I told her the story. Another band.

It had all gone so effortlessly. Bobby and Bob, and myself, for that matter, seemed to assume automatically that I was what they were looking for. A done deal. It was that unspoken thing once more. I was in. Again.

Of course, there was the rest of the weekend to think it over, and all day Monday at work. Part of me wanted to run screaming from the hall, but another part had already stepped right into the vortex. There was something about Bobby's concept that seemed like it might work.

Monday, I got home from work, packed my stuff, drank a cup of coffee, and made it to the Monroe Inn by five thirty. I couldn't believe I was doing that. I was in a daze.

Bob was already there, and he helped me put my stuff on the stage.

"Did you learn some of those songs over the weekend?" he asked.

"Yeah, not quite half the list. Are those other guys going to be here?"

"Here they come now."

A black guy was pulling a dolly full of drums through the door, followed by a white guy carrying a guitar case.

"Hey, Bob!" greeted the drummer. Then he noticed me. "Who's this? Is this our new bass player?"

"Yep," introduced Bob. "This here's Frank Siraguso." Then, to me, "This is Charles Sharrieff, the drummer, and Barry Johnson, lead guitar."

"Saraguzo, huh?" mused Charles. "Must be Eye-talian. Pleased to meet you," he said, as he flashed a winning smile and offered his hand. "I sure hope you do better than the last guy. He was OK, but he played like one long bass solo."

I shook hands with Barry. "Hi," he said. Charles was about six feet tall, good-looking, close-cropped hair. It turned out that Charles worked for the City too, as a meter reader for the Water Department. Even though he still had on his work uniform, he had an easy elegance of manner that made him seem like he always had on a tux.

Barry was shorter and heavier, but his longish black hair and pencil moustache made him look like Errol Flynn. I half expected him to strap on a fencing foil instead of his Les Paul. Made by Gibson, the Les Paul is the Rolls Royce of solid-body guitars, named after Les Paul, one of the inventors of the solid-body electric guitar and who actually did invent multitrack recording. Barry was reserved and had a dry sense of humor; Charles was more outgoing. Both had a businesslike, no-nonsense attitude about getting to work and helping me fill in.

Soon after, a stocky white guy with a dark-brown Beatle-cut showed up with two saxophones. Charles introduced me to Rufus Bailey.

Bob called the rehearsal to order. "Well, gentlemen, shall we get started?"

Charles set up his drums. Barry and I tuned up to Bob's keyboard, and had a beer. Then we ran through some of the material I had learned over the weekend. It was almost as if we'd been playing together all along, especially with Charles. He was such a good drummer, one who understood the music and how the drums and bass should interact to drive the band. Finally, we took a break after a few tunes.

"Hey, Frank! That's all right!" Charles was beaming.

"I always try to play along with the drummer, but you make it easy!"

"Man," said Charles, "if only we can stick together long enough, we'll have a tight band. I guess the next thing for us to do is teach you the show. It's not hard, but you have to watch Bobby's cues. And you have to use dynamics. You know, be able to go from loud to quiet and vice versa."

"I'm so glad to hear it! The other bands I've been in weren't like that. I mean, we were good, but it was just straight ahead rock. Blast out."

So, the work began. The Bobby Love Show was to officially open on Tuesday, March 22, 1978. They had about one month to teach me the show and bring the act together.

Charles, Barry and I worked at our respective jobs every day from eight to five. Barry worked in a warehouse. About five thirty or six, we would roll into the Monroe Inn and practice, usually until midnight.

Bobby would hang around for a couple hours while we worked on the dance set. Then he'd say, "I'll be back in about twenty minutes, I'm going to pick up Janine," his girlfriend, who also ran the spotlight for the show. The spotlight was a theatrical followspot, about three feet long, on a short, adjustable post and a base with casters. It had different colored gels, and the light beam could zoom from wide to pinpoint. The operator follows the talent, in this case Bobby Love, keeping him in the circle of light, and has to know the show inside and out and be able to keep up with any surprise moves. Janine was really good at it.

Every night we'd work on the dance sets and some of the show tunes, waiting for Bobby to return with Janine so we could work on the act. "Twenty minutes" always took about two hours. After a couple of nights, this wore a little thin. By the time Bobby was ready to rehearse the show, I was ready for bed. Near the end of the week, I was rehearsing lying on stage flat on my back, eyes closed. The other guys thought it was funny, but it worked fine for me.

Things were coming together quickly. The rest of the band had already been working together for at least a couple of months, so all I had to do was plug in my part. The dance sets were easy enough. We all just stood up there and played the songs. But the show rehearsals were serious work. Bobby had it all planned out, with every move and every song scripted and choreographed. As in live theater, everything hinged together and we really had to be on top of it. I was amazed at the quality

An Urgent Message

of the musicianship of the band, of Bobby's voice, and his rendition of Elvis.

In less than a week, I learned the whole show, more than thirty songs, and two dance sets, another twenty or so. Whew! That gave us three weeks to tighten up and be ready for our debut.

On weekends, until the show opened, we played the Monroe Inn as a regular band. It was just Charles, Barry, me, and Bobby with Joe, another singer, sitting in for some songs. This was totally unrehearsed and had nothing to do with the show, but was a way for Bobby to earn his keep while he used the Monroe Inn to ready his act. It also gave me experience working with Charles and Barry, which was a real help. In this configuration, Bobby played rhythm guitar. Actually, he played quite well.

The material was country-western stuff. We did no Elvis songs. Bobby called the tunes, most of which I'd heard, if not played. He'd call out the name of the song, and the key or first chord, and off we'd go.

The songs were structured, like so much popular and blues music, on the I-IV-V pattern. For instance, in the key of E the first chord, or I, is E. The second chord, or IV, is A. The third chord, or V, is B7. In the key of C, the chords are C, F and G7.

Bobby used an endearing method of communicating chord changes for songs we didn't know. "This means the first chord," he explained, holding up his index finger. "This is the fourth – the second chord," holding up two fingers, and, holding up three fingers, "this is the fifth." Then, holding up only his middle finger, "This means ya fucked up! Heh-heh!" So much for music theory.

That first weekend was easy money. The crowd didn't seem to care whether we fucked up or not. They had fun, so I guess we did OK. At the end of Saturday night's gig, it was time for Bobby to pay the band. After packing up our guitars, mikes, and snare drum – we left the amps and other things at the bar for the week's rehearsals – Charles, Barry and I went over to a table where Bobby was sitting with two other men, whom Bobby introduced to me as "Lee Miller, my personal manager," and "Ed Frazier, my manager."

Lee was definitely a piece of work. Looking rough and worn around the edges, Lee was maybe over fifty, had longish, thinning, grey hair with long, unkempt, bushy grey sideburns, steely blue eyes and a ruddy complexion. He looked for all the world like he had just stepped out of a Daguerreotype. The resemblance ended there. He wore a rumpled blue and white polyester disco-country shirt, and brown jeans. Lee stood up to shake my hand, saying, "H-how do you do." He had a bad stutter, and a southern Missouri or Tennessee accent. Lee, it turned out, handled the day-to-day operations of the Bobby Love Show.

Ed, who seemed to be about forty, was well-dressed for the Monroe Inn. He wore a black suit, white shirt and no tie. His well-groomed, jet-black wavy hair was slicked back, like Elvis, and he sported a Vandyke. He stood up and heartily shook hands with the new guy, and his barrel-chested form was a good two inches taller than either Charles or me. Ed, Charles and Barry exchanged greetings. Although he looked dangerous, Ed turned out to be easy-going and friendly, but not the kind of guy to fuck around with. He sat back down, took a drink from what looked like a whiskey and Coke, and then, to my surprise, pulled a fat wad of bills out of his coat pocket from which he happily peeled off what was due us. So Ed was the moneyman.

There were other details to take care of during the time before opening night, such as getting me a wardrobe for the show. Bobby sent me downtown to Sir Knight formalwear, where I bought a used pair of black tux pants for twenty bucks. They looked pretty good. Another day, on my way to work in the morning, I stopped at a tailor shop downtown to be fitted for the black, double-breasted vest that was part of our band uniform. The elderly seamstress had a shop on 12th Street up above the strip of sleazy bars between Central and Wyandotte that was a fixture for so long a time, until they were torn down to make way for a new hotel. I'd always wondered what was above those bars, and now, in part, I knew. She took my measurements and the vest was ready in a few days. It fit well and looked great.

Bobby also provided us with two ruffled tux shirts apiece. Each of us had a red one, which was the standard, or default, color we all wore for the big nights, like opening night, or Fridays and Saturdays. Our other shirts were of different colors. I had a green one, for instance, and Charles had a light blue one. These were for alternate nights. Barry's running joke was that the getup made us look like waiters. Sometimes he would throw a white bar towel over one arm and move through the crowd like he was going to take orders.

Throughout this time, rehearsals continued unabated, the weekend gigs rolled on, and I still worked my surveying job every day. It started to feel like the Bataan Death March. The show was taking shape, until we were down to our last week before opening. It was time for the full-dress rehearsals. Now we could tie all the loose ends together, nail down Bobby's costume changes and segues, and make sure we could go from start to finish without a train wreck. At last, I would see Bobby in costume and get the full visual impact of what it was I had jumped into.

The Bobby Love Show was divided into two parts: Elvis in the 1950s, and Elvis in Vegas, circa 1968. For the opening part of the show, the 1950s, Bobby had two costumes. One was a period-style tux jacket, pink with black trim, paired with black trousers with pink cavalry stripes down the legs, worn with a white tux shirt. The other costume was a gold lamé suit worn with a black shirt. Both outfits were well executed and looked great but, in the spotlight, the gold lamé suit was simply stunning.

For the Vegas portion of the show, which we did in conjunction with the 1950s set and reprised later in the evening as a separate show, Bobby had an array of jumpsuits, scarves and a pair of silver Elvis aviator sunglasses with amber lenses.

Jumpsuits. We're not talking about mechanic overalls here, or those funky things retired guys wear. These were faithful re-creations of Elvis' Las Vegas-era stage wear. And Bobby had five of them: Powder blue, dark blue, red and two white. All were made of the same double-knit polyester material. (In contrast, Elvis' suits were wool gabardine.)

The first four jumpsuits were of the same pattern, with high collars, zipper fronts, wide bell-bottom pant legs with wedge-shaped inserts of the same color extending from the cuff almost to mid-calf. Each suit was strewn with a seemingly random pattern of little brass stars, studs, and little mirrors, which were held on with Velcro. The mirrors reflected the spotlight back into the crowd like laser beams. This was a terrific effect but they had a tendency to fly off during performance, along with the occasional star. At the end of the night, the stage floor was littered with mirrors and stars, which Janine or Lee would gather up.

The fifth suit, white, was the Elvis Deluxe Rhinestone Extravaganza, nearly an exact copy of the suit Elvis wore in his 1973 Hawaii concert. It was cut from the same basic pattern as the other four, but had a higher, stiffer collar. Instead of stars and mirrors, it had a torso-covering American eagle done in red, white, and blue glass beads on both front and back. The front of the suit depicted the front of the eagle, and the back showed the back of the bird, which Bobby would often demonstrate to the crowd by turning around and spreading his arms like wings, much to their delight (ours too, but not for the same reason). Truly the pièce de résistance in the Bobby Love wardrobe. Bobby claimed he paid fifteen hundred dollars for the outfit and, for once, he probably wasn't exaggerating. Typically, Bobby wore the other suits during the week, and reserved this one for especially hot crowds on Fridays and Saturdays.

Each suit had its own matching Elvis belt. Made of the same material, the belts were wide, and had an enormous buckle, again of the same material. Both belt and buckle had the stars, mirrors, and glass beads, according to the suit. Overall, these were damn-near letter-perfect renditions of Elvis' costumes although Bobby didn't have that one belt with the giant silver buckle worn by the real Elvis, which looked exactly like a world championship wrestling belt.

Whichever outfit he wore, the gold lame suit, pink tux or jumpsuit, Bobby never appeared on stage without his Elvis wig. This was a necessary accessory because Bobby's natural hair, although black like Elvis', was curly, whereas Elvis had straight hair. Bobby had had this wig specially made, and it looked like Elvis' hair in late 60s to early 70s, rather than his original wavy pompadour and ducktail. Bobby's wig was sort of a longish Beatle cut, swooping down over the eyes, with sideburns that could be blended into Bobby's own long sideburns. Whenever he wasn't Elvis, Bobby kept the wig mounted on a Styrofoam head. On show nights, Bobby kept the wigged head in the dressing room, sitting on the makeup table next to his lighted mirror, a sight that never ceased to amaze and amuse us. All too often, one of us in the band would breeze into the dressing room and, seeing the wig out of the corner of an eye, stop short just before saying "Hi, Bobby!" to the wig. And sometimes we greeted it anyway.

The wig completed Bobby's image. Like his suits, it, too, was almost perfect, except for one little bitty detail, and one detail that many fans noticed no matter what town we were in: The wig was parted on the wrong side. Elvis parted his hair on the right side, and the wig was parted on the left.

I was dumbfounded at how many people picked up on this. The women and men who came to see Bobby were serious Presleyphiles, not to be duped. I asked Bobby about it once. "Yeah, it's true," he said, sounding glum, "but I'd already paid five hundred bucks for it, and it was too late to fix it."

Finally, we were ready for opening night, a Tuesday.

The show was due to start at nine. When I got there about seven thirty, an expectant crowd was already brewing. Soon, the rest of the Love Machine arrived, and we retired to the dressing room to suit up. It was crowded in there, too. The dressing room was really a small office/storage room, the walls incongruously covered in the same dark paneling so popular in porno movies. Besides Bobby with his costumes, his makeup table (which was really the office desk), lighted mirror, and the five band members, were a mop and bucket, and assorted cases of liquor. This was surely the Big Time.

To warm up the audience, the Love Machine went out and played a short dance set. The crowd was already buzzing and didn't need warming up. Then, we took a short break, turning all stage lights out. As he left the stage, Bob turned the jukebox back on. First rule of bars: Never allow silence.

After about fifteen minutes, Bobby sent word that he was ready.

Bob waited until we were all back on stage, still in the dark, then ceremoniously turned off the jukebox and climbed up on stage himself. A vibrant hush fell over the crowd. Bobby's mike stood alone on the dark dance floor.

An Urgent Message

Ready. Begin.

Still in blackout mode, Charles and I, drums and bass, started a low rumble, joined by Barry on guitar and Rufus on sax. When Bob started on flugelhorn, the audience recognized the first strains of the opening theme of Wagner's "Also Sprach Zarathustra," popularly known as the theme from Stanley Kubrick's movie "2001: A Space Odyssey." Everyone in the audience held his or her breath. The waitresses stood stock still in place. Not a drink stirred or glass tinkled. As the music swelled, so did the spotlight beam. By the end of 2001, Janine had brought the spot full up, and we broke into a vamp on Shake, Rattle, and Roll. We continued vamping, bringing the music down and under while Charles introduced the show.

"Ladies and gentlemen, through the magic of Bobby Love, we take you back to the nineteen fifties, when Elvis was the swivel-hipped king of rock and roll. We ask that there be no dancing, as this a floor show. So now, ladies and gentlemen, put your hands together for BOBBY! ELVIS! LOVE!"

Music up full. The crowd went wild. Janine swung the spotlight over to the dressing room door, and Bobby-Elvis emerged in full regalia: Elvis wig, the gold lamé suit, carrying an acoustic guitar. To ecstatic cheers, Bobby paraded around the stage to give everyone a look. Then went to the mike to sing Shake, Rattle, and Roll.

Women screamed, men cheered, everyone applauded. We'd only played the first song and the atmosphere was wild. We segued into another vamp and Bobby spoke as himself, the narrator, not Elvis.

"Thank you very much, and good evening ladies and gentlemen. I'd like to welcome you here tonight to my presentation of the Elvis Presley story.

"Basically, it all started in 1954 when Elvis, with the help of Sun Records, came up with a new and different sound. They called it rock and roll. And right now I'd like to take you back to 1954, when Elvis hadn't really developed the Presley style yet. But he was still turnin' the South upside down then, with the hit of sound of" – and here Bobby became Elvis again – "Baby . . . Baby . . . Baby . . . Let's Play House."

Two songs into the show and the crowd was storming with excitement. I couldn't believe it. But they loved it.

After "Let's Play House," Bobby continued his narration.

"You know, Elvis' career really started to move in 1955, when RCA stepped into the picture. But the kingpins of RCA were kind of skeptical about Elvis at first, and they were reluctant to take him to Hollywood. So they sent him off to Nashville, where he stood in the stairwell of a small, shabby studio, and recorded a song that skyrocketed him to the top of the charts in early 1956."

Bobby sang "Heartbreak Hotel."

Now the audience went nuts. This was way more fun than I thought it would be. And I was impressed with how Bobby paced the show. It's always one thing to rehearse a show, playing it through from start to finish and getting it down. It's quite another to perform it live for an audience, without a net, as it were. Bobby knew how to put an act together and not bore the crowd. Without waiting for the applause to end, he moved right along.

"You know, in the early nineteen fifties, until Elvis came along, it was really considered unusual for forty-five records to have good songs on both sides of them. And actually, back in those days, the kids didn't even listen to the other sides of the records they'd go out and buy. They'd just play over and over again the side they'd hear on the radio. So one day, as an experiment, a disc jockey played the flip side of "Hound Dog" on the radio. And, consequently, thousands of kids went out and bought records that they already had."

"Don't Be Cruel . . . to a heart that's true."

Bobby had 'em in the palm of his hand. We went straight into "Love Me Tender." By now, he had abandoned his guitar. For this slow tearjerker, Bobby took the mike from the stand as the spotlight softened to a deep blue and Barry began the opening riff. By the time Bobby ended with a powerful finale, there was not a dry seat in the house.

Bobby soaked up the applause as he put the mike back in the stand, and continued.

"You know, there's probably a lot of you here tonight that remember seeing Elvis on TV way back in 1956, on the Ed Sullivan Show. I don't care whether you admit it or not, it's been a long time ago.

"But you see, it really doesn't make any difference at all because, back then in those days, Elvis was always filmed on TV from the waist up." As he spoke, Bobby turned his hands palm-up at the waist and raised them. "So a lot of you never knew what was going on from the waist down." Still speaking, he turned his hands palm-down at the waist and lowered them. The audience was transfixed. "So I'm gonna show you."

There were whistles, applause and catcalls from the ladies. Bobby held on for a couple more beats and then, anticlimactically, shook his legs.

"That was it!" The tension broken, the audience laughed and applauded at the joke. On cue, Charles and Bob got into the act.

Charles: "Bobby, that was cooooool, man that was really cool!"

Bob: "But aren't you gonna show 'em the other part – part two?"

Bobby: "Part two?"

Bob: "You know, part two, the dirty part."

Bobby: "Say what!??"

Bob: "Part two, the dirty part, man."

Bobby: "Nah, I don't think I can do that tonight." Encouraging shouts of "Do it!" and "Let's see it!" flew from the audience.

Bob: "Are you kidding? This is opening night. I know you can do it."

Bobby: "I don't think I can do it."

Bob: "Now, Bobby, we've seen you do it, now we know you can!"

Bobby: "I . . . I . . . I can do it . . . but I have a headache tonight." Drum roll and rim shot.

Audience: "Awwww."

Bob: "Bobby, that is the best part, the people want to see it out there. You have got to do it!"

Bobby: "All right, I'll do it, I'll do it." He was resigned to his fate.

The audience cheered as Bobby took a stance at the mike. An expectant hush fell over the room. Bobby took his time. The Love Machine was silent.

Bobby, starting to shake: "It's comin', it's comin'!"

The audience laughed. Bobby hemmed and hawed, ruffled up and smoothed out.

"Ummmm . . . Here I come Baby . . . I think."

Bobby bowed his head and began to quiver all over.

"It's comin', it's comin'." He quivered a little more, then suddenly stopped, legs slightly apart.

Deftly, Bobby zipped his fly open and closed. The audience laughed, cheered, and clapped.

Bobby: "You missed it! No, as a matter of fact, you never would have missed it. No matter where you were in the building!"

Over laughter and applause, we immediately launched into "Jailhouse Rock." After an extended ending, the band went into a vamp. Bobby pranced around the stage – the dance floor – taking bows as the spotlight played on him and the crowd.

An Urgent Message

Exit Bobby. The crowd was ecstatic.

As we continued to vamp, Charles announced: "Ladies and gentlemen, the show is not over. That was just the first half. Bobby's making a costume change and will be back in just few minutes. He will show us what transformed Elvis from one of the most controversial figures of the 1950s to the most popular entertainer of all time. But first, we, the Love Machine, would like to do our theme song. It's called – The Love Machine."

We did our thing, each of us taking a solo. Then, we slid back into a vamp, and Charles continued his script.

"Ladies and gentlemen, we take you now to the Continental Hotel in 1969, where Elvis returned to performing after an absence of eight years."

We segued into "Viva Las Vegas." Bobby bounded onto the floor, resplendent in his powder-blue jumpsuit, Elvis belt, a white scarf, and those aviator sunglasses.

Bobby had told us that he had gotten the sunglasses from Elvis himself in Nashville, while riding an elevator with him.

"I told him I did a tribute to him, with his songs," recalled Bobby. "He said to me, 'You gotta lotta nerve, Baby.'"

So there he was. Elvis in Vegas at the Monroe Inn in Kansas City, and the audience was there with us.

Bobby didn't narrate during the second set as he did in the first set. Instead, it was a re-creation of the Vegas performance, complete with scarves to give away with kisses. Actually, the scarves were strips of polyester material, in various colors, cut to look like scarves. They weren't even hemmed.

Women really loved those scarves and kisses. They stood impatiently in line to get one of each, while Bobby's bodyguards kept things moving smoothly. One of Janine's jobs during the break was to put a mike stand holding a goodly supply of scarves on stage. Bobby would put a scarf around his neck, mop his brow with it, sweat on it, and then gently wrap it around the woman's neck while kissing her on the cheek. Or lips, if the mood and the woman were right. Some nights the mob was so thick, Bobby hardly had time to sweat on the scarves first, or kiss the girls afterward.

The set moved from "Viva Las Vegas" through "CC Rider" to "Suspicious Minds," ending with "Can't Help Falling In Love." And a lot more in between. The show lasted about an hour and a half, and still the audience wanted more. As we vamped, Bobby exited to a roaring, standing ovation. When he was off stage, Charles, as we kept vamping, announced that we were taking a break, but would be back soon for a dance set and another show. "So stick around."

During our twenty-minute break, I went over to the table where Anne and some of our friends were sitting. "Boy! He's good!" she crooned. "And that band is wonderful. A lot better than Foxfire." Our friends agreed. After break we played a dance set. The dance floor was packed.

As we played, I noticed a big, tall Mexican woman, probably in her twenties, dancing close to the stage. She was a good dancer. She was looking at me, watching. She smiled. I looked around, nervously. Yes, she was talking to me, all right. I smiled back. Then she motioned me down on the floor to dance with her, while I was still playing, no less.

No, I shook my head, not losing a beat. I turned to get support from Charles, but he was laughing too hard. Looking back at the woman, she was beckoning and laughing.

No! No! No! And I was laughing, too.

After another show, Vegas-Hawaii-style, and a closing dance set, we were done for the night. It was hard to get into the dressing room because Bobby was holding court there. Changing clothes was out of the question. The room was packed with people, mostly women, there to congratulate Bobby or get a kiss or an autograph or both. We tried to get our things and get out while women tried to latch onto us. Barry was inching his way out when he was cornered by the aforementioned dancing Mexican woman. She literally had him in a corner, her arms blocking his path.

"Hi!" she said sweetly, in a heavy accent. "I'm Lupe! Keess me, big boy!"

"No! No!" pleaded Barry, laughing, trying to think fast.

"Keess me, keess me, big boy!"

"Let me out! I gotta go!" Carrying his guitar and clothes, he managed to duck under her arm and scram.

"Wait! Come back!" she cried. "Keess me! Keess me!" He got away. She went over to Bobby.

"Bobby, keess me!" Before he could protest, she sat on his lap and planted a big one on him. Finally, arms flailing, he struggled free, laughing. "You gotta lotta nerve, Baby!"

That was some opening night. So it went for the rest of the week, and into the next.

Because Charles, Barry and I had to work in the morning, after getting home to bed at two in the morning or later, this schedule was murder. But it was OK. One handy feature of the Monroe Inn was that it opened into the Mexican restaurant next door, and the food was great. Sometimes I'd wolf down an order of four tacos before going home for the night. What I lacked in sleep I made up in tacos.

It was this opening period of the show that witnessed the birth of Frankie Stone.

At a certain place in the shorter, second Vegas act, as the Love Machine vamped, Bobby would introduce the members of the band. He called each of us by name, after which we'd acknowledge the audience and do a short solo flourish, about four bars or so. Not only was this a nice touch of showmanship, it was something Elvis did too. Sometimes, people in the audience would talk to us during break and it was surprising to us that they knew our names!

For the first two nights, Bobby's band intro went something like this:

"On trumpet and flugelhorn, from Kansas City – Bob Buster! On saxophone, from Kansas City – Rufus Bailey! On lead guitar, from Woodbridge, New Jersey – Barry Johnson! On bass guitar, from Kansas City – Frank Si . . . Sira . . . Straus. And, from San Bernardino, California – Charles Sharrieff!"

Bobby badly butchered my last name those first nights, and always looked back at me like, "Well, I tried."

On Thursday, I noticed a distinct change. So far, Bobby had played it straight with our names and hometowns, and I was starting to wince at his pronunciation of my name. But on this night, Bob Buster was from Las Vegas, Nevada, as was Rufus. Charles was now "the spark plug of The Love Machine," (and still from San Bernardino; Barry was still from Woodbridge, both true) and I, to my surprise, had become "Frankie Stone, from Newport News, Virginia." I almost wasn't sure he meant me, until he turned around to point at me, laughing. Certainly, the new intro made us seem more glamorous, and it was a lot easier to say Frankie Stone. Surely, it was a stroke of showmanship genius on Bobby's part, and I had to laugh too. Newport News? I'd never even been to Newport News, and still haven't. The new introduction stuck with us, and Bobby used it from then on. For a few nights after, though, I listened carefully to be sure he said the same names and places every time. He did.

Friday night of our second week at the Monroe Inn, Charles, Barry, and I were sitting around after the show, having a drink, cussing and discussing nothing in particular. Bob had already left. Payday wasn't until Saturday, but I, for one, was glad to be able to shoot the breeze and not have to dash home

An Urgent Message

to bed. For some reason, we weren't in the mood for tacos. It was almost closing time and the crowd had mostly thinned out. By chance, our table was near the men's and women's restrooms.

As we talked, I noticed a woman going into the rest room. I recognized her as the cute brunette who had been dancing all night without shoes. She was a petite woman, with long dark hair. Not long after a big, tough-looking Mexican woman – not Lupe – went into the rest room.

"Bobby says we're going on the road soon," Barry informed us.

"Oh yeah?" I asked. This was serious. "When? Fuck, I'll have to get ready to quit my job. I'm not sure I want to. I've been there a long time."

"Yeah," said Barry, "but I can't wait to quit mine. It's a drag, working in a warehouse."

"Well, I don't mind," offered Charles. "I didn't want to work for the Water Department forever, anyway. Frank, don't you work for the city, too? Man, won't you be glad to get away from there?"

"Sure, but I don't want to get away and then have this fall apart."

"I know, man," Charles empathized. "Look, I got a wife, and a kid too. But this is something I just gotta try. It's what I've always wanted. I did it for a while in California. Man, Frank, you'd love it out there. See what I'm sayin'? If we're good enough to dump ol' Bobby sometime, it'd be great. I mean, he's got a good show, but you can't do Elvis forever."

By this time, about ten women had gone into the rest room. I wasn't thinking anything about it, but it was getting obvious.

"Charles, I don't think any of those women have come out of the john yet. Is that right?"

"I don't know, Frank. You watching' the bathroom or

somethin'?"

"No, but it seems funny that none of them have come out. It can't be that big in there."

Just then, there were loud thumps and shouts from the women's john. The door slammed open. Someone was fighting to get out but other women blocked the way and they were all yelling and swinging. All we could see were asses and elbows.

The three of us watched in amazement. Although we couldn't really see anything – all the action was in the john – it looked like a hell of a brawl. A short, skinny man waded in through the john door to stop this female foolishness, reminding me of Popeye. He disappeared into the churning mass. More thumping and bumping. A minute later, he flew out the door and across the room, landing on his ass. The women went back to fighting amongst themselves. I looked at Charles.

"Is this the kind of place we always play?"

"I hope this is the worst," he said, glancing at the ladies' room door. "I don't see how it could be worse."

Barry called us to order. "Gentlemen, this looks like our cue to go home. Good night."

Bobby' show was so wildly successful at the Monroe Inn that Mike, the owner, extended the gig for another two weeks. We were starting to feel at home. Even the people at the Mexican restaurant knew us by name. I was getting the hang of working day and night and catching up on sleep over the weekends. During the gig, I would sometimes catnap in a dark corner of the bar during break. If I slept through just two breaks, for fifteen minutes each, that was an extra half-hour of sleep. A bonus!

As much as women were thrilled with Bobby Love, some guys weren't quite convinced. During one of our breaks, as Barry and I were making our way through the Monroe Inn's crowded tables, I picked up snatches of conversation. It re-

An Urgent Message

minded me of a comic strip in the Village Voice, "Stan Mack's Real Life Funnies," which promised, "all dialogue guaranteed verbatim."

Off to my left somewhere I heard one guy. His voice was deeper and louder than the others, sort of a country accent, and it cut through the background of people happily drinking and talking when he said, "Aw shit, he don't look like Elvis." I wasn't sure if Barry heard him or not. When we got to the bar and ordered our drinks, Barry turned to me and perfectly mimicked the guy. "Aw shit." We both cracked up.

One night while we were getting ready, Bobby told us to "look sharp because a photographer's coming tonight." He had casually mentioned a few weeks earlier that he wanted to have some photos of himself taken during the show and sell eight-by-ten glossies to the fans. I hadn't thought much about it, but it turned out Bobby was serious. Scarves, photos, what next?

The guy showed up that night with a woman he introduced as his assistant. They arrived from another time zone, like maybe a party at Playboy's Penthouse. He, smiling and personable, stood about five-eight, with short black hair slightly longer than a crew cut. He wore a dark-blue, checked tweed sport coat, black slacks, white shirt, dark tie and black horn-rimmed glasses. She, smiling and personable, was a stacked blonde number standing about five-ten, with hair coiffed in a French roll. She wore a tight-fitting knee-length, sleeveless, royal blue sheath dress with a leopard-skin collar and matching royal blue spike-heeled shoes. Va va voom!

During one of our breaks, the photographer took shots of Bobby and the Love Machine. While his assistant stood nearby nursing a drink, he got all the requisite band poses: standing together; looking serious; acting goofy; and individual shots of each band member holding his instrument (Charles held his drumsticks). The guy had Bobby pose some photos in costume and also got some action shots during the show.

A week later, he came back with the proofs. Some of us bought group and individual shots. Bobby picked out two action-Elvis shots, and ordered what seemed like a million prints of each and put them in cheesy, tan plastic frames. Janine, statuesque, gorgeous Janine, would prowl the audience during our dance sets hawking the pictures. They sold like hotcakes.

At last, the gig was over and it was time to bid adios to the Monroe Inn and the Mexican joint. We packed up and moved south and east a few blocks for a two-week stint at Genova's Chestnut Inn.

The Northeast News notes that Genova's opened as a jazz club downtown in 1933, and moved to 12th and Chestnut by the late 1930s. It became a landmark country-western club in Kansas City. Everybody who is somebody had played there at one time or other, often before they were anybody. Conway Twitty, Red Foley, Loretta Lynn, Kitty Wells, Wanda Jackson, Willie Nelson, Jerry Lee Lewis, Flatt and Scruggs . . . the list goes on. Their photographs were a hall of fame for all to see, covering the wall just inside Genova's door. This heavy, solid wood slab was encased in stainless steel. It had a bullet hole on the outside, below the porthole window.

And now, Bobby Love could take his place in the pantheon. Bobby's Elvis picture was stapled to a sandwich board sitting on the floor, surrounded by all the famous country stars.

Charlie Genova had seen a lot of trends come and go. While talking to us during a break one night, Charlie told us his theory of why Kansas City went from a flashy, swinging jazz town to a honky-tonk country music town. Both had coexisted for years in Kansas City but there was a sea change.

It was World War II. According to Charlie, as the jazz musicians and fans were drafted or moved to other parts of the country for defense work, people from the surrounding rural areas moved into Kansas City for the jobs left open. And they were fans of country music.

With all of that going for it, Genova's was definitely a step up from the Monroe Inn. Even the fights were more legendary. Genova's also had its own kitchen, which served steaks, Italian and Mexican food. In the mid-1950s, you could get a T-bone steak dinner for a buck twenty-five! Roberto, the cook, made some of the best burritos around. Barry and I loved them.

The Chestnut Inn also featured a special drink, The Buckaroo. Supposedly it originally had vodka, lemon juice, orange juice, pineapple, passion fruit and papaya juice, topped off with 190-proof alcohol. When we worked there it seemed to be a less-flammable combination of Hawaiian Punch, three kinds of rum, vodka, and whiskey. Whatever was in it, The Buckaroo came in a tall, vase-shaped glass and cost two dollars and fifty cents. A huge, crimson satin poster hanging on the wall at the back of the stage, right behind Charles, urged patrons to "Buy a Buckaroo and take home the souvenir glass!" It also noted there was a "limit of only two per customer," but by the end of any given night there were often many tables littered with empty Buckaroo glasses.

We used Charlie's office as our dressing room. The door was just to the right of the stage, from the audience's point of view. It was a small, dingy room packed with history. If only those walls could talk! There were two old shotguns in the corner by Charlie's ancient wooden desk, a closed-circuit TV showing the room – the bar area – so Charlie could keep an eye out for trouble, and more pictures on the wall. Taken in that very office, they showed such luminaries as a young Jerry Lee Lewis, sporting a moustache, sitting on the same old sofa we sat on. The sofa was still sitting in the exact same place, up against the wall near the desk. On the back of the office door was a giant poster of Hank Thompson. Although Barry greatly coveted it, he never figured out a way to make off with that poster.

Charlie was quite a character himself. He must have been at least in his seventies by then, but he never missed a night. He walked through the club talking to his customers, many of whom he knew by name, wearing his customary white shirt and black slacks that were always cut a little too high in the cuff. Whenever there was a lull in the music and dancing, he would stand by the stage and exhort us to "Play Proud Mary!" and then laugh. We laughed too, but we never played that song.

The Chestnut Inn had a reputation as a rough place – Charlie had seen fistfights, stabbings and shootings – but we never gave it a thought. For one thing, Bobby's cover – three dollars for singles, five dollars for couples – sort of kept the riff-raff out. More important, the Genovas – Charlie, his son Pete, and Pete's cousin Joe – kept a lid on it. They just plain didn't take any crap in their bar. True, there had been shootings, but it wasn't always the patrons pulling the trigger. The Genovas had no qualms about returning fire. Naturally, by the time the cops arrived there'd be no gun to be found. As far as the Love Machine was concerned, it didn't hurt that Pete and Joe liked the band. And we made sure to stay on good terms with them.

By this time, I had the show down pat and the Love Machine, as a band, was becoming tighter by the day. During our two weeks at Genova's, we played to a packed house every night and knocked 'em dead. The crowd really liked Bobby and the show, and they really liked the band, too. It was hard to get to the bar for a drink without having to stop at several tables along the way. Some women would reach out and grab us by the arm and start talking. It was fun chatting up the customers, but we had to make sure to get back on stage in time. Charles and I were talking to a group one night about where we were from and what we wanted to do. From several tables behind me someone said, "Aw shit, he don't look like Elvis." I looked around but couldn't peg him. It sure sounded like the same guy from the Monroe Inn. Maybe his wife or girlfriend liked the show so much she made him come to the Chestnut Inn too. I glanced at Charles but he was focused on the conversation.

The stage at the Chestnut Inn was smaller than the Monroe Inn's, but nicer. For one thing, it didn't look like a cattle pen. The front of it was brick, about four feet high, and it formed a little wall around the stage that made a handy footrest. Even so, it was cramped. We had the PA columns standing at each end, a microphone and stand for each of us, Charles' drums, Barry's guitar amp, my bass amp, and Bob's Fender Rhodes electric piano, which he played when he wasn't on horn. And let's not forget Rufus and his two saxes.

Then there was the low ceiling. The Monroe Inn had a high ceiling, maybe eighteen feet. Genova's ceiling was about twelve feet. When we were on stage, we could easily touch it. Because practically everyone in the bar (in all bars) smoked like dragons, our heads were in a dense cloud of cigarette smoke.

It may seem hard to believe, but none of us in the band smoked cigarettes. To make sure I wasn't the only one getting light-headed, I asked the others about it, and they confirmed. By the end of the first set, we were all reeling from the cigarette smoke we sucked in while singing. The best remedy was a shot of whiskey.

During the sets, Bob would scan the room, noting the plumes of grayish-white smoke rising from all the ashtrays. "Looks we've got a new pope!" he'd cheerfully proclaim. Few got the joke. Our clothes always reeked of the bar: old smoke and stale beer. It would all come back the next day at home, when I'd open my case to clean off my bass. Stale air from the night before would fill the room, as if I'd opened Pandora's box.

My bass would feel sticky and grubby from the smoke. Barry agreed and Bob added that bar smoke was hard on instrument finishes, especially brass.

One night, maybe Wednesday or Thursday, I got to the Chestnut Inn a little early. It was quiet and not many customers were there yet. I sat at the bar and asked Pete for a whiskey and Coke. Just then the phone behind the bar rang, and Pete answered. "Telephone for Louie Meyers," he called out, sort of smiling. He set the receiver on the bar and finished making my drink. From a table near the stage, Bobby came over and took the call. I tried not to eavesdrop. He spoke softly to the caller for about half a minute. When he hung up I asked, "Who's Louie Meyers?"

"That's my real name," he said. "But don't ever use it in public, 'cause too many people are after me," he said flatly, going back to his table.

As I sat nursing my drink, pondering the possibility of somebody whacking Bobby during a set, Charles strolled in. I hailed him to the bar and told him about the call.

"Is Louie Meyers Bobby's real name?"

"Yeah, that's right," Charles said, grinning. "It's Bobby's real name, but he doesn't like us to call him that."

After Saturday's show, at the end of our first week at Genova's, Bobby asked us to meet him at the joint about two Sunday afternoon to rehearse some new material. With some grumbling, we agreed. I mean, not only was it our day off, but two in the afternoon is kind of early for most musicians, and certainly for Bobby.

We all arrived about the same time. Genova's was empty except for Pete, who was cleaning up. In those days, bars weren't allowed to open on Sunday, so that was cleanup day. The joint's day off, so to speak. Pete let us in.

Being in a closed bar on a Sunday was always a little like

showing up for the aftermath of a wild party. When I was a little kid, sometimes my dad would go on a Sunday to the bar he was working at to help clean up or decorate for the holidays, and sometimes he'd take me. He worked at several over the years, with names like the Wander Inn and the Hideaway. There would always be some tables with empty beer bottles and glasses with half-finished drinks, the ice long melted. Stale beer, whiskey and cigarette smoke combined to form an atmosphere of decadence at rest. But what always got me was the dead quiet. The jukebox was off, the house band gone home, their instruments often left on stage, awaiting the band members' return on Monday or Tuesday. (Bars frequently had house bands that played for weeks, months or even years.)

And there was that lonely light. When the bar closed on Saturday night, the last one out, usually the bartender, turned out all the lights except for one or the odd neon beer sign. If the joint had any windows, the anemic daylight limping in on Sunday would cast forlorn shadows across the tables.

Bobby had some new Elvis songs for us to learn and he also wanted us to learn some new songs for our dance sets. Rehearsal was going well, but Bobby seemed distracted. We'd been at it about 45 minutes when Ed Frazier and Lee Miller showed up and called Bobby aside for a few minutes.

"C'mon, guys," said Bobby, "let's go unload this stuff."

What stuff? We all, the Love Machine, Bobby, Lee and Ed, went out to Genova's parking lot. There sat a root beer-colored Chevy van with Rich Roberts, owner of Rich Roberts Music, at the wheel. Rich got out and proudly opened the back doors. His van was packed with sound equipment. Somehow, Bobby had convinced Ed to spring for a new PA. So far, we had been using some nameless, piecemeal, mongrel setup for the voice mikes and mikes for Charles' drums. The speakers were small and sounded fuzzy. The system in general was ready for the crusher.

We crowded in for a closer look. It was a brand-new Peavey sound system, complete with new mikes and stands. It looked great. The smell of new equipment, better than a new car, wafted out of Rich's van. Rich grabbed a handful of papers and he and Ed went inside to sign Bobby's life away. Bobby picked up a couple of microphone cases, the smallest, lightest things available, and headed inside. The other five of us (the Love Machine, that is) teamed up to schlep the big stuff. There was a 12-channel mixing board and a power amp to run it. That would handle all the microphones we had and then some. And there were four huge speaker cabinets, each about four feet high, three feet wide, and two feet deep. Two cabinets were the bass speakers and the other two, which had big, white plastic treble horns, were for the high end. There were also six monitor speakers that we could set on the stage floor so we could hear our voices over the instruments. In addition, there was one of those newfangled Crumar string synthesizers, which were just coming into vogue. The Crumar was essentially a keyboard specifically designed to electronically create the sound of a string or horn section. It could also credibly mimic a piano or Hammond B-3 organ, all in a package that weighed a mere fraction of a real B-3. Although a B-3 is a great addition to a band, other musicians will go out of their way to avoid having to move one. With their wooden cabinet and foot pedals, they weigh a ton and are murder to carry. A guy could almost carry the Crumar under one arm.

We hauled it all in, set it all up, and took the PA for a test drive. It sounded great. The voices were so clear now. The new PA took up part of Genova's dance floor, leaving Bobby less room to move in the show, but it sounded so good and looked so neat that none of us cared. But it wasn't lost on us that we, the Love Machine, would also be the roadies.

We went over some new material, still in awe of the PA,

and took a break. Ed, Lee, and Bobby sat with us. Bobby announced that at the end of our Genova's engagement we would be going out on the road.

"How are we gonna carry that PA?" asked Bob.

"I've got a truck and trailer," said Lee. We'd seen Lee's truck, and weren't comforted at the thought of riding in it.

Bobby went over our itinerary. First, we'd have a week in Atchison, Kansas. From there, we'd play a week in glorious Minot, North Dakota, at a joint called the Torchlight.

This was scary. Finally, I had to make arrangements to quit work. I had been there five years, and had just been promoted to instrument man, operating transits and levels. All along, there had been rumors about the road, but I held off giving notice, just in case it didn't happen. When the time came, it caught me up short. I was nervous. There was only a week to go.

Fred, the chief of survey, didn't say much when I told him. In a way, I don't think he was too surprised. My co-workers were a little shocked, because I'd been there so long. They were also glad for me because nearly everyone's goal was to get out of survey.

He Don't Look Like Elvis

Atchison

On my last day at the City, Red, our party chief (leader of a survey crew), took a vacation day. That left me in charge. Instead of saying goodbye, he stayed home and gave me an easy day. Our current project was way up in the north part of the city, more or less out in the woods. We did what little work needed to be done, then cruised. It was a beautiful, sunny spring day. At the shop that afternoon, I said my goodbyes to my fellow surveyors and friends. Some of us had been through a lot together, and they wished me well. That night Bobby Love and the Love Machine were leaving for Atchison. We were hitting the road. It was Tuesday, April 25, 1978.

The touring company met at Genova's late that afternoon to pack up the equipment and stage our departure. By now, we had acquired another spotlight operator, Bob Hickerson, to replace Janine. She had been training him during our last week at the Chestnut Inn. Maybe she didn't want to tour with us (I wouldn't blame her), or couldn't. Barely 21, Bob was the youngest of the group. That made three Bobs: Bobby Love, Bob Buster, and Bob Hickerson. As we broke down the PA and other stuff, something dawned on me.

"Where's Rufus, Bobby?" I asked.

"Aw, he quit. He said he wanted four hundred dollars a week to go on the road, and I can't pay it."

"We gonna get another sax man?"

"No. For now, we'll have to do with Bob on horn and keyboards."

So we had one less guy to worry about, one less mouth to feed, one less to travel with. That's band life. Rufus was forgotten as we went back to the task at hand.

"He sure had some good dope, though," remembered Barry, staring into space. Indeed. Rufus asked Barry and me to smoke a joint with him on opening night before show time. Sure!

Barry and I laughed, just talking about it. "Man, I could hardly see!" he said. Same for me.

For our traveling comfort, Bobby had Lee Miller's pick-up truck-camper and a trailer to carry the equipment and all six of us. (Maybe it was a good thing Rufus quit!) The truck was a Chevy, white, about a '71. Beat to hell. Tennessee plates, long expired. Luckily, the trailer would hide them. The maroon trailer was the size of a medium U-Haul, and in much better shape than the truck.

We loaded the equipment into the trailer. This first time it was tricky figuring out the loading order and what fit best where. With all the stuff we had – the PA and all its speakers, Barry's and my amps, Charles' drums, the keyboards (have we forgotten anything?) – the trailer was bulging. In the coming weeks, we would hone the loading and unloading into a science. Speed is of the essence when you want to get set up and go eat or pack up and get home.

Finally, it was time to head out. I was kind of sad, and excited, and confused. Was I doing the right thing? We'd be gone two weeks. Then what? It was like stepping off the deep end. Anne got in the Toyota and drove off, waving one last time.

Bobby and Bob Hickerson sat in the truck cab, and we, the Love Machine, sat in back, in the camper. There would always be this distinction between Bobby and Bob Hickerson, and the band – Charles, Bob Buster, Barry Johnson, and me. It was a natural outgrowth of the organization, rather than any attempt at alienation or classification.

Any band gets tight by working and practicing together. The Love Machine was no different. The band members spent the most time together, rehearsing and working out songs, and in performance. We were on stage together all night for shows and dance sets. And we handled the equipment for the whole show, setting up and tearing down, although Bob Hickerson helped whenever he could. Among other things, he had charge of the spotlight, and we helped him set it up on tables, usually, or wherever it fit. It was a good team effort and we soon developed a working friendship. Bobby, being The Star and management, rarely joined in the roadie work. He worked out his end of the show with us, and did his performance, but pretty much went his way and left us to our own devices. We probably could have hung out more with him, but we were simply too busy. And by the time we had taken care of all the details, Bobby had left the building.

Bob Hickerson, on the other hand, was Bobby's de facto valet. He ran the spotlight, but also made sure the scarves were put on stage and took care of Bobby's wardrobe – the Elvis suits. These duties kept him close to Bobby. Then, too, Bob was single and ready for the partying that Bobby liked to do after gigs. It wasn't unusual to see them disappear with a couple of dames while we gathered up our instruments. Even so, we enjoyed Bob's company. He was smart, funny, and ready to discuss a wide range of topics. He would sometimes hang out with us in the afternoon, or go to lunch or dinner with us, whereas Bobby seldom did. It was rare to see Bobby even awake before three in the afternoon, whereas we tended to get up "early," around nine a.m., no matter what time we got to bed. It wasn't that we didn't want to hang out with Bob Hickerson, we just had different schedules.

It was murder in the camper. Bobby had it stuffed with all kinds of crap: Elvis costumes, old costumes from when he did a Tom Jones show (!), various shoes, the souvenir photos, the spotlight, his clothes, and clothes we had no idea whose they were. Not packed in any sense of the word. Scattered. Thrown in. Total disarray. On top of that was our luggage, horns and guitars! Any musician worth his salt keeps his instrument as close as possible. Neither Barry nor me nor Bob Buster, for that matter, would think of letting our instruments out of our sight, or trust their safety in that trailer. The camper was bad enough. And we wouldn't even think of leaving them in a club overnight, or even an afternoon. We perched as best we could on the wheel wells or wherever there was a spot in the midst of the debris. The camper wasn't tall enough for us to stand up and the bunk, which hung over the cab, wasn't wide enough for anyone to stretch out, and forget sitting up. We were hunched over and folded up. Fumes from the truck exhaust leaked in through the camper door. We were being gassed. To top it off, the door was screwed up and wouldn't close from the inside. It had to be padlocked from the outside. Trapped! On the plus side, the camper windows let in plenty of sunlight.

By the time we were well on our way to Atchison, something else was dawning on me: it was some 900 miles to Minot.

"Jesus," I said, "it's gonna be a long ride to Minot."

"No way," proclaimed Bob, "am I gonna ride in this motherfucker all the way to Minot, North Dakota."

"We'll die," added Barry. "I feel like a prisoner."

"I'm gonna do something," said Bob, "'cause this just ain't gonna cut it. We'll be lucky if the truck makes it up there in one piece."

"And you know Bobby doesn't have any insurance," quipped Charles.

"What would OSHA say?" I said.

"I'm going to see to it that Bobby rides back here, too," stormed Bob.

"I should have known," I said, dejected. We let the subject

die, sitting silent a few moments, listening to the sound of the road.

Then I continued. "Man, this has got to be bizarre! Today was my last day working as a surveyor for the City, and tonight I'm on the road with Bobby Love and the Love Machine! Who the fuck thought up that name?"

Barry laughed. "Charles did."

Charles laughed, too. "Yeah. Bobby asked me if I had a good name for the band. I didn't, so, you know, just kidding, I said 'the Love Machine' – Bobby Love, Love Machine, see – and he looked at me, and said, 'Great! That's it!'"

By the time we got to Atchison we were cramped, and smelly from fumes. When Bob Hickerson finally opened the camper door, we exploded out, gasping for air and stretching.

We'd arrived at the Melrose Motel. It may have been nice in its day, but the sun had long since set. Now some of the units rented on a monthly basis, like apartments, but the motel was still in business. It even had a swimming pool, which evidently hadn't been cleaned in years. It was full of dead leaves, and the water was black. We tried not to walk too close for fear that the Creature from the Black Lagoon would reach out of the water and drag us in.

The Melrose also had a nightclub, and that's where we would play. The office/club building was a long, narrow, cinder-block affair, with the bandstand at one end. The light-blue walls had a Wonder Bread wrapper motif – red, yellow, and blue balloons. Hell of a thing to see on a drunken night.

The owners were two slim, middle-aged cowboys who lived together in a trailer in back of the motel. Bobby, who seemed to know them, mentioned in passing that they were lovers.

Bob Hickerson went and got our keys. Bobby was staying with a friend in town. We had three rooms between us. We all entered one of them to check it out.

It was basic motel tacky, with beige walls and furniture. But clean. It would have to do. Barry wandered into the bathroom and peed. He tried to flush and then he turned the water on in the sink.

"Hey! You guys . . ." Before he could finish, Bob Hickerson broke in.

"There's just one thing," Bob said. We all turned and looked at Bob with an "oh, no" look. "There's no water. They said maybe by this weekend we'd either get water, or different rooms with water."

"He's right," groaned Barry, standing in the bathroom door.

"Are you kidding, man?" demanded Charles. "Didn't they know we were coming?"

I was indignant. "What the hell kind of deal is this? How are we supposed to shit and shower with no water? This is uncivilized!"

Bob Hickerson was defensive. Why, I don't know. We weren't blaming him for the message. "Well, there's nothing they can do. They accidentally gave our rooms to somebody else. The owners said you all could use their trailer to shower and use the bathroom."

"I'll bet they did," crooned Bob Buster.

"Yeah, don't drop the soap," chuckled Barry.

"Aw, man, this sucks!" I said. "Accidentally my ass! Why don't they put those other people here and give us our rooms back?"

"Because we're not paying customers," said Bob Buster, making a point.

We could have killed. We fumed a while. Then Barry spoke up.

"Bob, you say they'll have water or new rooms by the weekend?"

"That's what they said."

"Well, what do you guys think? I think we ought to commute from home until the weekend."

"Yeah, that sounds like the best idea to me," said Charles. "We could share the driving. But I hope they get us some water. And this weekend we're leaving for Minot."

"I'll do it," agreed Bob Hickerson "I don't have any water, either. Bobby's staying with a friend."

"Figures," said Bob Buster. "OK, it sounds good to me. I sure in hell don't want a room without water. Might as well sleep in the street."

"Great," I said. "OK, then, let's go set up for tonight."

"Frank, what are you doing home?" Anne woke up when I walked into the bedroom about four in the morning.

"Our motel rooms didn't have any water, so we're commuting until Friday. They said they'd get us some rooms with water by then."

"You're kidding!" she mumbled, before drifting back to sleep.

The show would be over at two a.m., and Barry, Bob Buster and I would throw our instruments into the car – we took turns driving – make the hour's drive with Charles and Bob Hickerson back to Kansas City. Next day, we'd meet about six in the evening and drive up to Atchison.

Finally, Friday came. Believing we'd have water, there were no plans to drive back. Bob Buster called early in the afternoon, and told me to meet him at his folks' house. Charles came to my place and Anne drove us up to Bob's. We found the place easily enough. Bob was waiting outside. In the cul-de-sac was a brand-new Dodge van. Red.

"What do you think?" asked Bob.

"Is this yours?" asked Charles.

"Sure is. I told you I wasn't going to Minot in that truck." Bob figured he could carry the keyboards, Barry's amp, his guitars, my bass, and our luggage, of course. We all carried a week's worth of clothes, plus our tuxes for the show. The van would take some pressure off the poor trailer. Charles and I put our stuff in the van. Bob had already packed his.

I kissed Anne good-bye, and she drove off.

"Now, all we have to do is wait for Barry," said Bob. It wasn't long, and we were on our way.

When we got up to the Melrose, we found that our rooms had not been changed yet. Still no water.

On Tuesday, our first night, I went into the bar's john during break. No stool or pisser. Just a hole in the floor with the standpipe exposed where the stool would be. It was cabinet à la Turk, without the footprints. Well, hell. I just pissed down the pipe. So that's what they thought of their customers.

For all that, the show had been going great all week. The joint was crowded. Some fans had even driven up from Kansas City. There was also a rumor that some guys were going to punch out Bobby as he made his entrance for the show. It was only natural. Guys were jealous because their girlfriends and wives were falling for Bobby, making their boyfriends and husbands buy those souvenir pictures. Just in case, Bobby had his bodyguards ready. He always hired a couple of local big-boys for the occasion. Mainly, they kept the women in line while Bobby handed out scarves, but they were really there to stop trouble.

After the show that Friday, we changed out of our tuxes and then sat around visiting with customers and drinking. We didn't have to drive back to Kansas City, and it was nice just to relax. Because the Melrose was a private club, it closed at three a.m.

In Kansas at that time, there were bars that could serve only three-two beer (3.2 percent alcohol) and private clubs that could serve the full spectrum of booze, wine and five-percent beer. The three-two beer joints were open to anyone 18 and older and closed at one-thirty a.m. The private clubs were open to anyone 21 and older and closed at three a.m., but there was a catch. You had to be a member to order a drink. Membership fees were usually low to encourage business (a dollar, two dollars or so). The whole system was a royal pain, and in the mid-1980s Kansans voted to eliminate the private club law.

Barry and I were talking to Cindy and Roxy, who had driven up from Kansas City to see the show. They were sisters who had been coming, often with their mother, to see Bobby Love since we started at the Monroe Inn, and we had gotten to kind of be friends with them. Cindy was a year or two younger and not as svelte as Roxy, but she was smart, down to earth, and fun. (Years later, she would own a biker bar in Knobtown, east of Kansas City.) Roxy, on the other hand, was a blonde vixen of five-two. A hot and sassy dame. She and Bob Buster had a brief fling while we were at the Chestnut Inn. Coming in one evening to get ready for the gig, I saw Roxy kissing Bob goodbye. After she left, he came over to me as I was putting my bass on the stage and said, happily, "You know, some women are just made for fuckin'. Man, is my dick sore!"

"You guys sounded better here than you did at the Monroe Inn," said Cindy. "We're gonna come back tomorrow for the Saturday show."

"Sounds good," I answered, "thanks. Say, are you two hungry? I think Barry and I are going to eat somewhere."

Roxy declined. "No, we're going home. I've got to work tomorrow."

"Too bad," I mourned, with crocodile tears. "We'll see you tomorrow night."

They left, and I turned to Barry. "Let's go see if we can

find Bob and Charles."

Bob was sitting at a table with Janine and her cousin Jane, his new flame.

"Hi, Janine, Jane" said Barry. "Bob, do you want to go eat?"

"Sure! Where at?" After all, it was almost 4 o'clock in the morning.

"I don't know. We'll see what we can find. Have you seen Charles?"

"Lightweight. He went to bed already. Jane, do you know any places open?"

"I'm not sure what's open now. I think there's a burger place downtown."

"I don't care what it is," continued Bob, "as long as they got food."

"Good," said Barry, "'cause you're driving."

We piled in Bob's van. Barry and I sat on the floor in back. The only two seats were the driver's and shotgun, occupied by Bob and Jane. Bob cruised through the deserted streets of Atchison.

"Go down to the light and take a right," directed Jane. "I think the place is on the corner."

Jane was right. There it was on the corner. Closed.

"Closed!" cried Bob. "The motherfucker is closed! What kind of town is this ain't got no all-night restaurant? What time is it?"

I looked at my watch. "Four o'clock. Boy, that's too bad. And I was looking forward to a BLT."

"What do you think?" said Barry. "How about that place we passed on the way in to town?"

"What," I said, "you mean that place that said EAT, made out of a reconstituted streetcar?"

"Yeah, well . . . "

"He's right!" agreed Bob. "We need food!"

Off we went.

It was a few miles out of town across the river on the Missouri side. Only place on the narrow, two-lane highway, middle of nowhere. No lights anywhere, except the lights on a tall pole shining up on the sign, the one bright spot in the deep night visible for miles: EAT.

We pulled in. There was one car on the gravel lot.

The interior was soaked in the sharp, harsh glare of fluorescent lights. This was not an Edward Hopper painting.

Across from the entrance a counter ran the length of the car, and to our right the end of the dining car was expanded to add a small room with four tables. A woman, maybe 60, wiry and not very tall, stood behind the counter cleaning and wiping. A man in a cook's apron slouched in the kitchen doorway in the back wall, just past the counter end. He looked a little older and was probably the woman's husband. They had to be the owners. Who else could they get to run the joint?

We sat down at a table. Across from us sat two couples, maybe in their thirties, out to sober up. From the souvenir pictures and scarves the women held, we knew they had been to see Bobby's show. The women seemed bubbly and happy. The men were quiet and sullen.

As we looked over the menu, the waiter came up to the table. He was a big guy, dressed in jeans and chambray shirt, like the men at the other table. He had a speech defect, though, which made him sound like he was holding his tongue while talking. Somehow, I took him to be the owners' son.

"May I take your order please?"

Barry went first. "I'll have a tenderloin and fries."

"Our fryer is turned off," the waiter informed him.

"So you don't have any fries or anything?"

"Un-unh. That's right. We got hash browns, though."

Barry studied a minute. "OK, I'll have a hamburger and hash-browns."

Jane's turn. "I'll just have a Coke."

"We're out of Coke. Got Sprite."

"OK, Sprite. Large."

Bob ordered. "I want ham and two eggs over easy, and biscuits."

"We got sausage, no ham or biscuits now. Toast."

At this, Barry and I started to chuckle at the cosmic design of it all. Bob gave in.

"All right. Give me sausage, two eggs and toast."

"Over easy?" Bob nodded yes, and the waiter turned to me. I played it safe.

"I'll have toast and coffee." The waiter got it all down, and left. "Boy," I went on, "I think half the menu was shut down."

Barry had a story. "That reminds me of this place in Florida. It was run by this old Cuban guy. He was a nice guy, but he didn't hear too well, or didn't speak English too well, I don't know. But anyway, you'd give him your order, and he'd smile and shake his head 'yes.' Then, when he'd bring the food, it wasn't even near what you ordered. It was nuts! I don't know why he even bothered to have a menu. Or even take orders! All you'd have to do is walk in, and he'd bring whatever he thought you wanted."

At that delirious hour, this seemed real funny to us. We were still laughing and talking when the waiter came around with the coffee pot. He filled our cups and one guy at the next table called him over.

"Why don't ya pour me some more coffee there, cousin?" This man had been eyeing us as we talked. The more fun we had, the more he disliked it. Bob and Jane had their backs to him. Barry and I were facing him and his group. In my old neighborhood, when a guy said "cousin" or "cuz" like that, you knew there would be trouble.

Finally, he set his cup down hard, and snarled at Barry. "So you think that's funny, Slick? Ya wanna be introduced?"

Barry looked over at him. "Yeah, I'm talkin' to you, Slick. You think that's funny, laughin' at a poor guy that can't talk right? Ya think that's funny?"

Barry was nonplussed. "What? I'm not laughing at him."

"You were so, I heard you. You think that's real funny, don't ya?"

The other man intervened. "Come on now, Bud. Those guys aren't laughing at him. Leave 'em alone."

"Bill's right, Bud," said the woman with Bud, "they don't mean no harm. They're just having a good time."

Bud was not convinced. "Now, goddammit, they was laughin' at him." Then he turned to us. "Y'all think that just because you're from the city you can come out here and make fun of us country people. Well, you're wrong. If you think it's so funny, why don't you step outside in the parking lot and we'll see who's funny!"

The woman behind the counter had been watching warily. Now she spoke out, irritated. "Bud, hush up! These people don't mean no harm, now let 'em be!" Naturally she knew these guys.

Bud turned to her. "No! They can't laugh at him like that." Then to us, "Come outside, we'll settle this right now!"

"Now, you can't do that," stated the woman. But nothing doing. Bud struggled to get out of his chair, but the others at the table tried to hold on to him. Bud broke loose and stood up, but his chair was in the way. He attacked it, kicking and cussing, while the others tried to calm him.

As for us, we had no interest in fighting someone easily twice our collective size, which Bud was, who was hung-over to boot. Not to mention his friend. We got up and started backing toward the door.

"Well, just get out then," growled Bud, voice rising. "Go on! Just get out! I'll pay for your breakfast, but get the hell out!" Maybe he would have let us get it to go . . .

"It's all right," the woman said to us. "Go on and stay. Your food'll be out in a minute."

"It's not either!" cried Bud. "I said get the hell out and I meant it!"

We took his advice. Bud continued kicking the chair and pounding the table. In the parking lot, getting in the van, we could see Bud still abusing the furniture. Just as we were about to leave, a Pinto pulled into the lot. It was Janine, with Bobby riding shotgun. He rolled down his window.

"Hey Bob, how was it in there?"

"Oh, man, don't go in there" he warned. "There's some guy who was gonna rearrange our faces for us."

"What the fuck for?"

Barry leaned out Bob's window, "He thought we were laughing at his cousin with the speech defect."

"Were you?"

"Fuck no, man. What do you think? Would you?" said Barry.

"Heh-heh. So he wanted to whip you, huh?"

"Well, we're leaving," said Bob. "You do what you want. But I wouldn't go in there if I were you." With that, Bob pulled out and headed back to town. I watched through the van's side mirror. Janine followed shortly. It was raining lightly.

Back at the Melrose, Bob pulled the van down around behind one of the buildings, out of sight. We went to his and Barry's room. Bob and Jane sat on the floor, and I sat on a chair. Barry was on his bed. We were mulling the situation over. We were a little worried about being followed, but were more concerned about having one more night to work. What if Bud and company showed up for Saturday's show, and recognized us?

"Boy!" exclaimed Bob. "That was close. They shouldn't see the van hidden behind the building."

"I'm still hungry," I griped. "We never did get our food!"

"Jesus, what a great place," Bob went on. "Eat. It was bad

enough they didn't have anything on the menu, but then the clientele!"

Barry had their number. "Yeah, they were all pissed off because their girlfriends, or whatever, made 'em go see Bobby Love. And then made 'em buy those pictures!"

"They were pretty mad, all right," agreed Bob. "But I don't think they knew we were in the band, or I think they'd a killed us for sure!"

"I hope they don't try to follow us," said Jane.

"Well, if they follow us, at least I'll be ready for 'em," said Barry. "I brought my two friends along . . ."

Reaching into the gym bag he always kept nearby on stage – it held things like guitar tools, cords, strings and a flashlight – Barry fished out a thirty-eight.

" . . . Smith and Wesson."

"God-damn!" Bob and I cried in unison.

"I didn't know you had that," I marveled.

"Yeah, I keep it on stage" he said. You never know when you'll need one."

"Fuck, I'm glad tomorrow's our last night here!" said Bob.

"I'm glad to know we have some cover if we have to shoot our way out!" I said. I wasn't just thinking about the Melrose, but of any clubs we'd be working!

Saturday was our last night. That afternoon, we got rooms with water. Big deal. At least we could shower. Bud and his pals never showed that night. There wasn't any trouble at all. It was a good finale, and the crowd loved us to the end. Ed Frazier and his wife, Willa, came up from Kansas City to catch the show, pay us for the week at the Melrose, and see us off to Minot. We decided to pack up and hit the road right after the show, because Minot was such a long ride. It was almost five-thirty by the time we were ready. We had gathered the vehicles by the pool for a final briefing. The eastern rim of the sky was just starting to lighten.

"Well," said Bob, "we're on our way to Minot."

"Why not Minot?" quipped Barry. Nyuk nyuk.

"How far is it?" asked Charles.

"It's about nine hundred miles, I answered. "That'll take twenty hours or so. But it's got to be better than the Smelrose."

We mounted up, and rode off into the morning.

Minot

THE CARAVAN STOPPED FOR breakfast in St. Joseph, Missouri, at a Denny's. It was right off the freeway, I-29 north, which would take us clear to Fargo, North Dakota. Although I can't say I'm a big fan of Denny's, after Atchison it was Mecca. They had everything we ordered! Coffee, eggs, bacon – you name it. And plenty of it! After breakfast, we rearranged our seating. Charles and Barry went with Bob in the van. I went with Bobby and Bob Hickerson, whom we now called "Hollywood Bob."

Hollywood? Besides running the spotlight and being Bobby Love's valet, Bob Hickerson's other job was to sell those souvenir color photos of Bobby for four dollars apiece during our dance sets. Bobby gave him a percentage of the take, and he seemed to do well with it, considering. Even though he looked nothing like Janine, Bob had a knack for hawking. One night at the Melrose, during break, he had come up to Barry and me, laughing. He had on a polyester "disco" shirt. It was pale blue, with a picture of an Egyptian in a chariot on the back.
"I was going through the crowd selling pictures," he said, "and this guy says to me, 'Hey, Hollywood, where ya goin' in that shirt?'" From then on, Bob Hickerson was knighted "Hollywood Bob," or just plain "Hollywood." One less Bob to worry about.
Hollywood drove the first shift out of St. Joe, I had shotgun, and Bobby slept in the back, in the camper.
I woke up after a welcome, if cramped, nap. Par for the front seat of a pickup. The road looked pretty much the same as

when I had nodded out. Nothing in all directions. It was hard to gauge how long I'd been asleep. I looked at my watch. It was almost noon. I'd slept about three hours.

"Where are we?" I asked Hollywood.

"We're in Iowa." He fired up a joint.

"Very far?"

"A couple of hours."

"Then we're not even near Minot?" I asked, hope against hope.

"Ha! No way!"

"How we doing on gas?"

"We probably ought to get some soon. None of the gauges work, you know."

Great truck. No speedometer, gas gauge, heater, or horn. Lights worked, though. The odometer had stopped at thirteen thousand. More likely, it was a hundred thirteen thousand. Jeez, maybe two hundred thirteen thousand!

Interstate 29 follows the Missouri River Valley. The Iowa land there is so flat in all directions that we could almost see the curve of the earth. Nothing stood higher than the occasional house clear to the horizon. After endless miles of this flat farmland we passed Sioux City, Iowa, on the Missouri River. At some point, the highway took an upward turn. It was so subtle, I didn't notice until I looked in the outside mirror to check the trailer, and saw that we were now quite a way above the valley. The sun was shining, and the blue sky was dotted with low-flying puff clouds. Their shadows marched across the valley floor. There was a constant rush of wind as we drove ahead.

"Damn! Look at this view," I urged Hollywood, still driving.

"Wow, you're right! It's like flying!"

The narrow highway rose straight and pretty out of sight. It ended in the distance on what seemed to be a wall of hills.

I watched the valley recede. When we were too high and far away, I turned my eyes forward to watch as we neared the crest of this long-assed grade.

We broke over the top and into another world.

The land changed from flat farmland to glacier-scrubbed, undulating, treeless hills with ocean waves of tall grass. The Dakotas, ancient land of the woolly Mammoth.

A large sign proclaimed, "WELCOME TO SOUTH DAKOTA."

Soon after, we passed another sign promising gas at the next exit and followed Bob's van off the highway. We drove about half a mile on a winding, hilly road to find a remote outpost, a little general store with a gas station. There was one small pine tree near the place, striking against the barren, early-May hills and bright, blue sky. The trail of the lonesome pine. Gas, pop, and pee. On our way.

Traveling in the pickup truck was proving to be slower than we would have liked. For starters, the trailer hitch on the truck's bumper was loose. At highway speeds this made the trailer sway more than it would have normally. The thin safety chain connecting the trailer tongue to the truck frame did little to inspire confidence. There were visions of the trailer breaking loose and careening off the highway or, worse, having it come through the camper during a sudden stop. (Another reason not to ride in the camper.) Due to the weight in the trailer, it was hard to go much faster than fifty, unless we were going downhill with a tail wind. This we knew, even without a speedometer, because Bob was tracking us, constantly needling about going too slow. Whenever we did get up to fifty-five (the maximum highway speed in those days) the trailer was apt to start whipping violently back and forth. Like the tail wagging the dog, the whipping trailer would make the truck shake and weave, scaring the bejesus out of Hollywood and me. To stabilize the rig, we'd slow down to about forty or forty-five, and then build up speed again. Sometimes the trailer rode smoothly at cruising speed. Other times a bump or wind gust would send it flailing. Even though I-29 is a four-lane divided interstate without the worry of oncoming traffic, it was almost impossible to pass anybody. We were afraid that the trailer would start flailing and smack the car we were passing. Hampered as we were, there were those drivers who poked along even slower than the truck, and we had to pass them. We did the best we could under the circumstances. Bob was really impatient with this situation, since he could cruise at any speed in the van, but it was pointless to lose us. Without any gauges, we needed him to know when to stop for gas. We all needed each other to help navigate once we got into North Dakota. Had he beaten us to Minot, he could've done nothing but wait anyway, because, supposedly, only Bobby knew where the motel was. So it went, then. Speed up, slow down. In a word, torture.

By late afternoon, we were still heading north on I-29, still in South Dakota, probably somewhere north of Brookings. Low on gas, hungry, we pulled off to a truck stop. Not exactly what we had in mind, but it was the only thing we had seen for many hours and miles.

Built on top of one of those rolling hills, the truck stop was the only sign of civilization as far as we could see in any direction. One of those clean, modern buildings, circa early-1960s, it had lots of aluminum and glass, with floors and walls a mosaic of little square tiles of blue and white. We gassed up and pulled over to the restaurant. Hollywood went to unlock the camper door to let Bobby out.

"What if we just left him in there?" suggested Barry. We all laughed. It was too tempting.

A row of booths along the front window provided a nice view, such as it was. They were all full. The six of us sat at the counter, with our backs to the outside. We scanned the menus.

"Hey, Charles, they got tenderloins!" I taunted.

"Get outta here, man. You know I don't eat that swine!" A Muslim, Charles did not eat pork, drink alcohol, or smoke.

Looking over the menu, I speculated, not altogether idly, "I wonder if half the menu is closed like Atchison?"

"Oh, man, I hope not. I'm hungry!" exclaimed Bob.

"Well," said Barry, "I think a burger looks like the best bet."

"But look at this!" I cried. "Shrimp poor boy!"

"I'm dubious," said Bob. "Who in South Dakota would know about 'shrimp poor boys'? I mean, hell, everybody knows it's po' boy, not poor boy."

The waitress appeared. Everybody ordered hamburgers. Thinking of Anne's relatives in Biloxi, I went for the poor boy.

"We're out of shrimp," she informed me. So much for my exotic tastes.

"Mmmmm, cheeseburger, fries, and a Coke." She left. I turned to Charles. "I should have known better. Six months between airdrops and all. As if they'd ever had shrimp!"

The burgers weren't quite as big as we would have liked. Had we known, we might have ordered a double. But the fries weren't too bad, and a Coke is a Coke, pretty much.

It was a little after four by the time we finished and went outside. We convened on the truck hood to look over a map and plan our route. It was a few more hours up I-29 to Fargo, North Dakota. From Fargo, the obvious route was I-94 to Bismarck, some 200 miles west, and from there U.S. Highway 83 went pretty much straight north 110 miles to Minot. Although I-94 probably had more gas stations, Bob, Charles and Barry thought it would be faster to get off I-94 at Jamestown, a mere 97 miles from Fargo, and take U.S. Highway 52, the hypotenuse of the Jamestown-Bismarck-Minot triangle. Because, as we all know, the hypotenuse is shorter than the sum of the two legs of a triangle. It made sense, at least on paper.

Hollywood took a turn at the wheel, with Bobby up front and me in the camper. We mounted up and drove off. The afternoon sun in the clear blue sky pulled us on.

It was impossible to get any rest in the camper. There was just no place to sit for hours on end with all our stuff heaped all over. It was an obstacle course just getting in and out. The only clear space was up in the bunk hanging over the cab. It was up high enough that we needed help climbing in, but there was no ladder or anything solid to stand on. The only way was to grab the edge of the bunk and hop in, taking care not to bang one's head on the camper ceiling. Easier said than done. If we couldn't fully stand up in the camper, we certainly couldn't sit up in the bunk. The space was hardly more than two feet high. No laying on one's back with the knees up, either. And the bunk was too short for stretching out. The mattress was thin, and the sheets dirty from not having been washed. As the sun set, it got colder and darker in the camper. I was fully dressed – jeans, shirt, hooded sweatshirt, my traveling boots – and was still cold. There were only two positions in which to lie: the fetal, or an "L," with my feet hanging over the edge. The fetal position was warmer. For extra warmth, there was also an old chenille bedspread, threadbare and dusty. I pulled my hood over my head, the bedspread over that, and dozed intermittently, waking to look out the bunk's small passenger-side window, so thoughtfully provided by the camper manufacturer, into the deepening gloom, shivering.

Around seven that evening, I felt the truck pull off the highway and stop. Surely, I knew, rescue was imminent. Hollywood opened the camper door, and asked if I'd like to trade places with him.

"Where are we?" I asked, climbing out of the camper, still in a cold daze. The sun had set, the sky was dark.

"We just got on to I-94, past Fargo." I grunted comprehension. "You want to drive?" he continued. "I thought I'd try to get some sleep."

"Sure, I'll drive. Good luck on the sleep, though."

Hollywood got in the camper, and I locked the door behind him. Bob had stopped his van in front of the truck, and I went up to his window, to confer about our next exit at Jamestown. Settling that, I took the wheel of the pickup, greeted by Bobby as I got in. We were off again.

As we pulled out, Bobby and I got to talking, our first chance in a while. Bobby lit up a half-smoked joint.

"Did you hear me shooting back there a ways?" he asked.

"No," I said, surprised. "What was going on?"

"There were some ducks in a pond near the highway, and I fired my pistol at 'em, heh-heh."

"I didn't hear anything. It must have been one of the few times I was asleep. Did you hit any of 'em?"

"Naw. I fired about three or four shots, but don't think I hit anything."

"Too bad. What kind of pistol you got?"

"Just this little thirty-two." He pulled a small pearl-handled automatic from his leather coat pocket. It looked sort of like a Walther PPK, but was not. I told him about Barry and his two friends. He showed no surprise. "Well," he said, in tacit agreement with Barry, "you never know what might happen when you go on the road."

We talked about music, the show, what each of us had done, and our personal lives. He asked me about being married, and my old job. I asked Bobby if he had ever been married, and he said no. I asked him about Janine, how long they'd been together, and why she didn't go with us. "Well, she's got a day job and didn't want to leave."

Bob was so far ahead of us that, even with the light traffic, it was hard to tell which set of taillights was his or someone else's. With the odometer broken, we had no way to tell how far we'd come from Fargo. Our only hope was to follow Bob but we couldn't keep up with him. The exit came up suddenly and I missed it. Neither of us had seen a sign.

"Hey," said Bobby, "is that Bob taking that exit?"

I looked. "Gosh, I guess. Is that the right exit?"

By the time we noticed, it was too late to follow him. We drove on about five miles, using the highway mile markers to guesstimate our distance, until we found an exit where we could turn around. It took maybe twenty minutes or half an hour to catch up to them. I drove as fast as possible, balancing speed and the wild trailer. Bob had pulled over when he noticed we weren't behind him. They had begun to wonder what had happened to us, when we found them.

Later that night, about eleven-thirty, we figured it was time to gas up again. Hollywood was driving now, I was up front again and Bobby was safely locked in the camper. Hollywood and I both agreed it sucked back there. It was colder than the cab which, remember, had no heater. We figured, let Bobby sleep. And leave the driving to us.

Highway 52 turned out to be a pretty narrow and curvy hypotenuse. And pitch dark. We hadn't seen anything for miles, not even light from a farmhouse. According to the intermittent road signs, the next town was several miles ahead and a few more off the main road ("main" being a relative term). Wing, Turtle Lake, I don't recall. It might not be on the map. We figured it would be our last stop before Minot. Our concern was wasting gas on a wild goose chase to a town that had none. But we sure didn't want to run out of gas on that dark, lonely road! Without a gas gauge, we could only guess how much we had left. We guessed we were too low not to chance it.

Hollywood pulled up alongside Bob's van – we hadn't seen anyone else on the road – and I rolled down the window, hollering over to Bob that we had to have gas. He did too. Making our detour, we made it to the town with our fingers crossed. The town was, of course, rolled up and shut down. We split up and scouted around but found no open gas stations. Or anything else open, for that matter. I mean, this was late Sunday night (or, by now, early Monday morning) in a small town. We were discussing our situation at our rendezvous point. Our only other option was to park and sleep until morning when the gas stations opened. Just then a police car pulled up.

"Good evening," said the officer, rolling down his window. "Are you folks out of gas?" He was young, red-haired, and had that "North-country" accent. This seemed a familiar problem to him.

"Yes sir. We couldn't find any stations open," said Hollywood.

The officer chuckled. "Yeah, they're all closed. But follow me – I've got a woman in a station wagon full of kids waiting at the Standard station."

He wheeled his squad car around, and we followed. It was just two blocks to the station, one of the closed ones we'd checked out. We pulled in behind a red station wagon full of kids, who mugged and waved at us.

"Wait here," said the officer, "I'll go get the owner."

He returned a few minutes later with the owner, an old guy who followed in his pickup truck. Obviously, he'd been asleep. He was in his robe. Meanwhile, we had let Bobby out of the camper.

It was a relief to hear the gas tank fill. It was right behind the seat, and gas fumes momentarily filled the cab. We all gassed up, and waved good-bye to the kids in the station wagon as they drove off. Bobby paid the owner and gave him an extra ten-spot for the service. After thanking him and the nice officer, we were on our way again. That's America for you.

It was still a long damned way to Minot. We made one

more pit stop at a handy, isolated wide spot on the side of the road. It was cold enough to see our breath. I looked up to the sky and saw some pale blue clouds that flickered on and off. I thought it was just my eyes, blinky and tired from riding. Only later, in Minot, would I figure out what they were.

A little before three in the morning, we hit the outskirts of Minot. We spent some time driving in circles trying to orient ourselves, find our motel, and then find something to eat. We stopped for a roadside conference. Hollywood took the time to check the truck out.

"Look at this tire!" he exclaimed.

"What is it?" said I, who had a vested interest in such things. We all rushed to look. There was a bulge the size of a softball on the side of the left rear tire. Who knows how long it had been like that? Bobby was unruffled.

"Ahh, it's OK. It hasn't blown yet, heh-heh. We'll get another tire later." The truck's spare was worn past the tread to the chord. Hollywood and I decided to chance it on the bad tire. We drove as slow as we could.

More circles. Finally, we found an all-night diner. Not a chain, either. It was the real thing, with knotty pine walls and counter that gave it a hunting lodge atmosphere. We went in. It had been almost twenty-four hours since we left Atchison. We all were numb, but in good spirits.

Everything on the menu was available! I had pancakes and eggs over easy, with bacon. Oceans of coffee. Heaven! To make it better, Bobby was feeling expansive and picked up our tabs. The waitress pointed us to our motel, and we found it easily enough. We had already driven by it several times.

The Sandman Motel. The road sign was a man in the moon wearing a nightcap. We each had our own room. Bobby and Hollywood took adjoining rooms, as did Bob and Barry. That left Charles and me. This set the pattern for the rest of our touring: Bobby and Hollywood, Barry and Bob, Charles and me.

I went into my room and looked it over. Running water! That alone put it over the Melrose. The bathroom was clean, even if it didn't have that paper band around the toilet lid. Nice and simple. Bed, dresser, chair and TV. Like the restaurant, the rooms had that old-fashioned knotty-pine paneling for that rustic touch.

There was a door between our rooms. I opened it to see Charles' place.

"Damn, Charles, look at this! You got a kitchen! A stove! A sink! Fridge! Home! The lap of luxury!"

"Yeah, man. Now I can keep juice and good food around. I won't have to eat at those awful restaurants so much."

"Well, you wouldn't mind if I keep some stuff in the fridge?"

"No, Frank, I know you like to eat well, too. Go ahead."

I must admit to jealousy, but I'd live with it. I was silently marveling at the place when Charles said:

"Frank, why don't we change rooms?"

"What? What do you mean?"

"I mean let's change rooms. You move in to here."

"But why?" I didn't suspect his motives or anything, but why drop a good deal? I said as much to him.

"Because," he explained, "everybody will be in here using the kitchen, partying, smoking dope, drinking and carrying on. I got to get my rest, and I can't with all that going on. You don't mind that stuff like I do. You move in here." I must say, Charles did lead a tight life.

"You're not kidding?"

"No, man! I said take it!"

I thanked him profusely. What could I say? "Well, you can certainly use the fridge. I'll even cook for us, if you want."

"You Eye-talians and your cooking!" We laughed, and made the switch. Charles went to his room and closed the door.

It was quiet in the room, sometime after four in the

morning. I sat at the kitchen table and rolled a little joint. I felt a long way from home.

After an all-too-brief sleep, I was up before nine and had some coffee. That kitchen was a godsend. We went to the Torchlight club to get ready for that night's opening. We set up our gear and rehearsed a little. The club was in downtown Minot, which seemed like a lot of small-town downtowns. There were older brick buildings, and some newer ones that were built maybe in the fifties. Minot in general had few tall structures, hardly any over five stories. Unlike many larger urban areas, Minot is clean. The town is spread over the rolling, treeless prairie. Nearby are an Indian base and an Air Force reservation.

Despite the small-town atmosphere, the Torchlight was surprisingly uptown. Dark red, diamond-patterned carpeting reached up the walls. There was a large dance floor from which the small, two-seat tables tiered upward, so everyone had a good view. Each table had its own little lamp for that romantic effect. High-ceilinged, airy, it lacked the reek of stale beer so common in bars. In short, a regular nightclub!

Most important to us, the stage was very large. We were in heaven. Most clubs' stages are hardly big enough for the band's equipment, let alone the members. But here, we could spread out. Breathe. I could use both of my bass cabinets! I put one speaker, with the amp head on it, near me and Charles, and the other one on the far side of the stage for Barry and Bob. Stereo!

Opening night, Monday, wasn't so hot. We were all punchy from the long drive. And the crowd was thin. Plus, the Torchlight's size made the crowd seem even smaller than it was. We kicked off the intro of "Jailhouse Rock" just fine, but when Bobby sang, nothing happened. His mike was dead.

I could see his lips move, but heard nothing. Oh, shit!

There was nothing for the band to do but keep playing. That's the most important point to remember. Amps can blow, singers can collapse. Earthquakes, tidal waves. Just don't stop playing and it will be all right.

Hollywood left his spotlight post, and ran down to fix Bobby's microphone. He got it working just in time for Bobby to finish the song with us. It did slow momentum. Nonetheless, that was the only glitch, and we acquitted ourselves nicely the rest of the evening. The sparse crowd was politely appreciative.

The next day, Tuesday, we rehearsed at the Torchlight with Bobby, tightening up the show. We made some good improvements, as evidenced in the show that night. Late Wednesday morning Barry, Charles and I rode downtown with Bob to rehearse again for about an hour or so. After that, we checked out the town. Charles went to the local YMCA to exercise. Bob, Barry and I walked round. We found an amusement parlor, as it was called, where we played pinball and some video games. Some local teens were in there too.

Arriving back at the Torchlight, we decided to go to the liquor store in the basement before heading back to the Sandman. The Torchlight's main entrance was on the street and there was a back entrance in the alley, with a stairway down to the liquor store.

Before we could buy anything, we were surprised to find an entrance to another bar at the back of the liquor store.

We went in for a look-see and sat at a table near the back of the room. This joint, which didn't seem to have a name, was totally unlike the Torchlight upstairs. Much smaller, with a low ceiling, it smelled like a bar. Smoke and stale beer mingled in the air. Although it was early afternoon, it was dark as night. The only light came from the stage up front. Loud, cheesy music blared from a ratty speaker.

It took a few minutes for our eyes to adjust so we could take in the surroundings. All around were young guys like us, but dressed in boots, jeans, western shirts, some jean jackets and hats. Most were sitting alone at a table, some in twos or threes. Single-mindedly, each one gazed up at the stage. We followed their line of sight to a blonde, naked woman. She was dancing to the music, her clothes strewn about the stage floor.

"It's a titty bar!" cheered Bob.

"What the hell!" said Barry. We were laughing. What had we stumbled into?

What a scene. We stared in amazement. A waitress, fully-dressed, came to the table and distracted us long enough to take our order. Whiskey and Cokes all around.

When the music stopped, the woman stopped dancing abruptly. Without bowing or other acknowledgment, she gathered up her clothes and exited, still naked, stage right (our left) to polite applause, stepping down four stairs and slipping behind a black curtain. Like the crowd at the Torchlight above, this bunch was restrained and quiet. No whistling or catcalls like one would expect in this kind of joint. Another woman, a brunette, immediately came from behind the curtain, mounted the stairs and took her place. Both of them were tall and quite good-looking. They, like the rest of us in the place, seemed to be in their mid-twenties.

The new woman went over to the opposite side of the stage to a record player on a small table and put on a forty-five record. She had shoulder length brown hair, with just a hint of wave. She was dressed in jeans, a white, short-sleeved blouse, and brown, open-toed high-heeled shoes, as if she'd just walked in off the street. Neat and clean, but not fancy.

She did a strip dance, after a fashion, to the music. Neither she nor the blonde paid much attention to the beat. Really, they didn't even seem to be good dancers. Or they just weren't trying. When the record ended, she stopped dancing in midstream. It was jarringly unceremonious and matter-of-fact. She stepped over to the player to put on another record, returned to center-stage and resumed her dance. The record player did not even have an automatic record changer so the dancers could play a stack. The records were strewn about the table, with some on the floor. By the end of the second number, she was nude. Nekkid. Well, except for her shoes. With a few ungraceful moves, she had danced out of her jeans and panties without taking her shoes off. The stage floor was plywood painted black. It must have been rough on bare feet. Then again, those high heels were a nice touch.

Like her earlier colleague, her facial expression was blank, her demeanor devoid of humor, irony or any emotion. She made no eye contact or any attempt to communicate with the audience. She appeared to have what combat soldiers refer to as the thousand-yard stare. As each record ended, she stopped and changed it, dancing nudely if not lewdly through a few more discs.

"Look at this!" I said sotto voce to Barry and Bob. "She has to change her own damn records!"

By now, we had put back a few rounds and were bathing in the ambiance with the rest of the boys. Gazing up at the dancer, something caught my eye.

I nudged Bob. "Is that what I think it is on her nipples?"

"What do you mean?"

"I think she's got Scotch tape on her nipples." He looked at me askance.

"Whaaa...?" He looked for himself. "I can't see any tape." He was dubious.

"Well, you gotta catch its reflection in the light."

He looked again, squinting. "You're right! Barry! Look at this!"

It was true. One cellophane tape X on each nipple glistened in the spotlight whenever it hit just so. Removing it must have been less than pleasant. Why she wore it, I don't know. Some North Dakota law? A Minot ordinance? Maybe wearing tape meant the dancers weren't technically nude. And to top it off, she had to spin her own records! Well, that pretty much sealed it. We'd had enough watching that woman dance for those young cowboys, and we didn't have any free tickets to Bobby's show for her and the other dancers, so we finished our drinks and split. Hit the liquor store on the way out.

By then, it was time to pick Charles up from the Y. He got in the van, looking very worked-out. "It was great," he beamed. "I played basketball."

A gloomy, soft rain was just starting to fall, and the air was chilly.

As we drove off, I noticed a familiar figure. "Hey, isn't that the dancer we left with the boys?"

"Yeah," said Barry. A quick look passed between him, Bob and me.

"We could give her a ride," I said.

"Nah," said Barry. "She'd think we were mashers."

We looked on in silence as the van rolled by. We felt a sad sort of kinship with her. She was walking down the street, head bowed in the rain. Fully dressed and alone.

Thursday, we had to find a tube for Barry's amp. He had an Ampeg VT-22, with two twelve-inch speakers. It was small, but a heavy sumbitch. The tube had gone out during the last set of the previous night, leaving Barry with no punch to his sound. We looked all over town, in electronic shops, music shops. It would have been bad news not to find one. At last, someone pointed us to the good music store in town. Yes, they had the tube! Last one. Lucky find. The only one in Minot. Thirteen dollars. Jeez!

We had a better crowd that night, although Bobby wasn't exactly packing them in. By and large, the customers were well dressed, as if for a cocktail party, and polite. No hooting and hollering that was so prevalent in the Kansas and Missouri bars. The women waiting in line for a scarf and a kiss from Bobby were patient. They might as well have been waiting in line at the bank. No pushing or shoving, so the bodyguards had it easy. Everyone was having a good time and enjoying the show, mind you, but it was just hard to tell. Even the guys in the titty bar were quite reserved.

However, Bobby Love had a certain magnetism. . . .
That night, as we left the Torchlight for the motel, we ran into Bobby. He had a woman on each arm.
"Hey, you guys, hold on."
"Bobby, what's going on?" asked Charles.
"I want you to meet some friends of mine, heh-heh. This is Pinky" – a bottle blonde with dark roots and rabbit-fur jacket – "and Roxy" – stringy-haired brunette in a black vinyl jacket (not Roxy from KC). Both had on lots of makeup. Both were quite drunk. Bobby was in good spirits himself and having fun.
"This is my band," said Bobby, making a broad gesture at us. Pinky and Roxy smiled wanly. "Well, guys, we're going to be late for the party. See you later!" Bobby waved as they swept out the door.
Once back in Bob's van, we laughed.
"Man, he sure can pick 'em," said Charles.
"I think we're pretty lucky to miss the party," said Bob. We didn't seem to have been invited.
"Well," said Barry, "I don't know what they see in Bobby. 'He don't look like Elvis.'" Heh-heh.
We left the Torchlight and went to the all-night Safeway. Yes! An all-night grocery! The first, and almost last, we would see on tour with Bobby. No need to look for late-night restaurants like EAT. We had a kitchen and a fridge. Of course, we made the most of it.
Charles was right. As he had predicted, we tended to congregate in my room after the show each night to relax and eat.

It was great, not having to find an open restaurant all the time. Anne had made me some granola to take on the road, but we'd all gotten something from the store. Barry, Bob, and I had gotten some bread and lunchmeat for sandwiches. Also, thinking ahead, I bought a couple of chicken potpies for lunch or something. Charles showed a fondness for Kipper Snacks, which I like too. I showed him how to soup them up with lemon juice and pepper. Certainly, Hollywood and Bobby would have been welcome to join us, but they tended to eat out.

A knock at the door interrupted us as we prepared our midnight snack. We all looked at each other. We weren't expecting company. More insistent knocking. Charles, sitting closest, went and opened the door. From the table, where we sat, we could tell it was a woman, but not who she was. Charles was handling it, anyway.

"Frank, come here," he said.

Hmm, I had a feeling. I went to the door and Bob followed.

It was Pinky and Roxy. I opened the screen door.
"Is Bobby in there?" asked Pinky.
"No, he's not here," I said. "Did you try his room?"
"Yeah, but he's not there."
"Well, didn't you all leave the club with him?" asked Bob.
"No. We're in my car, and he said he'd meet us here."
"But he's not here," continued Bob.
"Well," asked Pinky, "can we come in and wait for him?"

Bob and I looked at each other. Charles had stepped back, washing his hands of the situation. Bob and I had the same first thought: Tell them to get the hell out. "You gotta lotta nerve, Baby!" I thought.

On the other hand, what do you do when two drunk women show up at your motel room at two a.m. in Minot, North Dakota? Hell, maybe they brought a party with them. But my nerve center said no.

"Awe, I don't know, we're all going to bed soon."

"Oh, come on," whined Roxy. "He won't be long."

OK, I let them in. Pinky and Roxy sauntered in and sat at the table. They'd had more to drink since we'd seen them last, and Roxy brought a half-pint of whiskey with her. Passing Jupiter, heading out.

"Do you know Bobby?" Bob asked Pinky.

"Yeah," she said, with effort, "we met him a couple years ago up here." Bob tried to keep up the small talk, but no go. Pinky and Roxy were too wasted to talk. And they kept casting what-are-we-doing-with-these-jerks glances at each other. Funny, we were thinking the same thing.

Half an hour, one joint and more booze later, still no Bobby Love. I was getting fidgety.

"Was Bobby going somewhere before coming here?" I asked.

"Nah," slurred Pinky. It was becoming clear. You can be anywhere in Minot in fifteen minutes. Bobby had given Pinky and Roxy the slip.

"Well," I asked, "do you know any place where he might be?"

"No," Pinky said. She reached for her cigarette in the ashtray. The butt was long cold. "Damn! Roxy, do you have any cigarettes?"

"No, they're in the car."

"Mine are in my purse . . ." She looked around and under the table and chair. "Shit, it's out in the car. Roxanne, I'm gonna go out and get my purse."

Pinky stood up, steadied herself, and tottered out to her car. Charles opened the door for her, gracious man that he is. Roxy decided to follow. I guess she wanted her cigs, too.

"I don't know . . ." she mumbled on the way out. Roxy seemed dubious of waiting for the Star.

"Come on, let's wait for him," I heard Pinky say from outside. "He said he'd meet us!"

"OK, OK," Roxy said.

Pinky's car was down a few doors, by Bobby's room. In their condition, it would take a few minutes. I watched through the screen door. They got to the car and started rooting around, looking for their purses. No sign of driving off.

An overwhelming impulse hit me.

I didn't even stop to question it.

Quickly, quietly, I locked the screen door, then shut the main door and locked it too. Then I turned out the lights.

"All right, you guys," I commanded the other three, "get into Charles' room and turn out the lights. Move!"

We rushed into Charles' room. Peeking out from behind the curtain over the picture window we could see the women walking back to my door. The others snickered. It was hard not to laugh.

"Silence!" I ordered in a hoarse whisper.

By now they were at the door. Pinky grabbed the screen door handle and pulled, expecting it to open. It was locked. She looked at Roxy.

"Hey, what the hell?" cried Pinky. She knocked on the door.

No answer.

She knocked louder. "Hey! Open up in there! I know you're in there!" They both called for us to open up. I felt kind of bad, but not that bad. I guess I could have let them back in. But I really didn't want to, and the others didn't either. They knocked and hollered for a few minutes, then went back to Pinky's car, where they sat and watched the door. After about ten minutes, Pinky started the engine, backed up slowly and drove away.

"Boy," exhaled Bob. "I guess Bobby dumped those two gals."

"No doubt," said Barry. "You know he's not coming back

here." We sat in the dark a while and talked, with only the light from the Sandman sign coming through the window. Pinky and Roxy didn't come back.

Neither did Bobby. Not that night, anyway.

He did show up next afternoon, with Hollywood. Barry told him the story of Pinky and Roxy, and asked Bobby if he knew them. He laughed.

"Yeah, I met 'em when I was up here about two years ago," he grinned. "The bass player got the clap from 'em, heh-heh."

Friday night saw our best crowd yet. Typically, they were well dressed and reserved, a few Air Force people. It wasn't that they were old. By and large, they comprised the usual age spread of Bobby's crowds.

During a break, we slipped down to the titty bar for a drink. Nothing had changed, except there were more boys and the air was smokier. We didn't see any of the dancers hanging out where we could talk to them.

Back at the Sandman, the band convened at my room again, after hitting the Safeway. A band travels on its stomach. Eating was our best entertainment. By the time we got off work, TV stations were off the air. Most of the audience worked in the day, so there wasn't much late partying, unless we counted Pinky and Roxy. (We didn't.) Earlier in the week, two women had given Barry and me their names and hotel room numbers. We were surprised because they didn't look like our type. Maybe it was their navy-blue suits and white blouses with big bows. Somehow, I pictured them offering us lemonade and cookies. Looks are deceiving. Maybe it would have been spiked lemonade and cookies naked. In any event, with no way to get there, we didn't make it.

After a couple of joints, our talk drifted to old movies, especially old monster movies, which Barry and I loved. I asked if any of them had seen "One Million B.C." starring Raquel

Welch. None had, but the story interested them. Or maybe it was just Raquel.

Saturday was our last day. We thought we'd take it easy. Charles met a woman in the Torchlight Friday night who said she'd give us a free pizza where she worked. Naturally, we wanted to look into it. Around noon, Charles and I got ready, and went over to Bob and Barry's room. While waiting, we turned on the TV. Look what just started – "One Million B.C."! Pizza could wait. The movie certainly lived down to its expectations. We hooted comments and worked up a good case of the munchies watching Loana (Raquel) and Tumak (John Richardson) fend off dinosaurs and cave dwellers.

Charles' new friend was behind the counter when we got to the pizza place. If she didn't look old enough to get into the Torchlight, the perky brunette could certainly charm her way in. The place was decked out like a circus tent. It had jukeboxes to listen to, and TVs to watch, with bowls of popcorn on the tables to be munched while waiting for pizza.

We looked over the menu and decided. Charles was sent to the counter to order. He came back too soon.

"She says the manager is here today, and she doesn't know if she could do it."

"Oh, man, Charles," groaned Bob, "I'm hungry!"

"Yeah," needled Barry, "where's this free pizza? Here, have some stale popcorn."

In a few minutes, the woman came to the table. "I'm sorry, but the manager is here today, or I'd give you a pizza. But you can still order one, if you don't mind paying."

"Well, we'll think about it," Charles said. She left us to the menu. It took us about thirty seconds. We left. Nobody wanted Minot pizza that much. Certainly not enough to pay for it. We went to our Minot standby: Sirloin Stockade. Mmmmm, steak, sort of. We'd already checked out the Mexican restaurant earlier in the week. Just as we thought – there hadn't been a

Mexican within a thousand miles of the place.

That night, the show started an hour early, at eight o'clock. That was because the bars had to close at midnight. Can't drink on Sunday. At every other place we worked, Sunday didn't start until one-thirty a.m., at the earliest. Or I should say, Saturday night didn't end until one-thirty. Not so in Minot. Midnight on the dot. Anyway, we got off early. Right after the show we packed the equipment and went back to the motel to get ready to leave. In what would turn out to be our typical modus operandi, we decided not to wait until morning. Why hang around just to sleep? We gathered in Bobby's room at the Sandman so he could pay us for the week.

"By the way," he added offhandedly, "you guys owe me three percent union dues."

Up to this time, at the Monroe Inn, Genova's, the Melrose, Bobby had never asked for union dues, nor had any union rep approached us. If the union would have gotten to us anywhere, it would have been Kansas City. Now all of a sudden, Bobby wants union dues.

"What? Who says?" asked Bob, incredulous.

"What do you mean? I thought it was two per cent!" exclaimed Barry.

"Well," Bobby explained, "the union's business agent told me they needed three percent." Who among us had a calculator?

"I tell you what," I said, "we'll work it up and pay you later." Fuck this, I thought.

"OK, OK." He was disappointed. "Don't wait too long; I gotta pay it."

We left and went to my room.

"That motherfucker," said Bob. "The union hall was right across the street from the Torchlight. I never saw anybody from the union. And they would have talked to us the first day, not the night we're leaving! That asshole was trying to fleece us!" It was an interesting lesson. Cheap, too. Bobby never got his three percent, and he never brought it up again.

We were road-ready by three a.m. Bob and Barry were near death with colds. Bob especially. He was nauseated, also.

"Here," I said, reaching into the fridge, "try some celery. It might help your stomach."

"Well, OK." Almost immediately, he felt a little better. He was amazed.

As we mounted up, I took one last look at the clear night sky. The sky up there was a continual source of fascination for me. It seemed much closer to the ground than in Kansas City. There were those pale-blue clouds again. They were always there at night. One night earlier in the week, as I watched them, they seemed to fade in and out. I thought my eyes were playing tricks again. Then, they suddenly blinked off and on several times, quickly and definitely, like fluorescent bulbs. I knew what they were then. The northern lights. Well, hell's bells, I'd never seen them before. These weren't as dramatic as I'd seen in photos, but cool anyway.

All in all, the Minot gig was a success. We were tightening up the show, and the crowds were enthusiastic if not big. Still, we – even Bobby, for whom home was where the show was – were ready to head on back to Kansas City. It was a long ride back. The coming Tuesday we had to be in Chillicothe, Missouri, to play at a joint called Duke's.

This time, I was in the van. Bobby hadn't even thought of getting a good tire for the truck. I made sure to ask about it before we pulled out of Minot. No, it hadn't been fixed. I informed the group that since I had risked my neck on the way up, someone else should try it on the way back. Charles volunteered. They all thought I was a little squirrelly, but I was adamant. No doubt, working for the City had made me safety conscious.

Barry slept in back while Bob and I rode in front. We drove south on U.S. 83 out of Minot, down across Lake Sakakawea, on the Missouri River. None of us wanted to retrace Highway 52.

It was nearly five a.m. when we got to the intersection of Highway 83 and I-94, just north of Bismarck. There was a Country Kitchen restaurant hard by the freeway entrance. We stopped to eat. The Kitchen was your typical twenty-four-hour chain, serving primarily breakfast, but also lunch and dinner. It was sort of like a Sambo's or Denny's, but had a better menu. They were one of Bobby's favorites. He especially liked the Clam Hopper, a fried clam sandwich. I had tried it at the Country Kitchen in Minot. Not bad. But at that early hour I wanted bacon and eggs, hotcakes. Coffee. Not clams.

By six or so, we were back on the road. It was getting light, the sun was rising, but the sky was cloudy and the air was damp and chilly. Barry went to get more sleep in the back of the van. We took I-94 east, Bob driving. I offered to drive a spell, but he said he liked driving.

"I once drove for twenty-six hours, while I was on the road with Tommy Riggs. Did a lot of cocaine." We, poor souls, had no cocaine. Save for joints and coffee, it was direct drive. Since joining the show, this was the first chance Bob and I had to have more than a passing conversation, other than shoptalk.

Already, Charles and I were becoming fast friends. We talked more by virtue of the fact that we were the rhythm section and roommates. I was still learning the fine points of the show, and I looked to Charles when I got lost. He was always there, in control of the beat. Also, he really was from San Bernardino, California, and we often compared and contrasted the West, which has much better roads and highways (no winter!), and Midwest, which has better barbecue.

Charles was the next oldest band member, and also the only other one married, although Barry had been living with

Debbie for a couple of years. Charles had a son about a year old. Spiritually, we had some parallels. He was a Muslim, of the Nation of Islam, and I had begun practicing Buddhism about four years earlier. The Muslims referred to themselves as Bilalian, rather than black, or African-American. Charles said that was the ancient name for the people.

In accordance with Islam, Charles didn't eat pork or drink alcohol. I, however, could eat what I damn well pleased. Also, Charles had to pray five times a day facing the east. To that end, he always asked the motel owners which way was north. Since we had gotten to Minot so late – or early – he had asked me that instead when we got to the Sandman.

I took him outside, showed him how to find Polaris using the Big Dipper, and pointed north. Then I asked why north and not east, since that was what he truly wanted.

"Well," he explained, "if I asked which way was east, they might think I was some weirdo. But north seems more harmless. And if I know where north is, east is easy." This did have a left-handed sort of logic to it.

"Maybe I'll bring along my Boy Scout compass for you," I offered.

I hadn't talked to Barry that much either. Barry's relatively quiet demeanor hid a very funny, dry, slightly twisted sense of humor. However, I did notice that Barry had a rare trait among lead guitarists. Rather than play one long, loud lead solo through each song, he knew when to vamp and comp. That is, he knew when lay back and play chords and fills, integrating his playing with the whole band. Then, when it was time to solo, he stepped up and kicked ass.

At first, Bob appeared to be the brash young arranger, cornet and keyboard player for the show. Bobby had actually hired him as the bandleader. As I was learning the act, at the Monroe Inn and Genova's, Bob would cast burning glances when I would fuck up. Which actually wasn't all that often, considering. Musicians, as are any people who work hard to perfect their skill and talent, are tough on those who seem lax in holding their own. Their treatment of incompetents can be downright cruel. I know. I've done it myself. That's why the old-time jazz players would have cutting contests. All of us also had to sing, too. We sang backup for Bobby during the show, of course, and sang the songs for the dance sets. Charles had the smoothest voice by far. "Like melted butter," said Anne's friend Cindy. He did most of the announcing, and his singing left the ladies limp. The singing was easy for me, especially once I had the show music down. By the end of our stint at Genova's, I had everything down. I was just another journeyman.

Bob had just turned twenty-two that April – an Aries. Barry is a Cancer, and I Gemini. Charles, Hollywood, and Bobby, I never did find out. They never mentioned birthdays while I worked with them, and I damn well wasn't going to ask them what their sign was. It seems that Hollywood had just turned twenty-one before he joined the show. That I remember, because he was happy he could finally buy a legal drink. So he could be an Aquarius or Pisces. These signs are noted as a public service. Charles was twenty-six, Barry twenty-five, and Bob twenty-two. Just. I was twenty-six. In June I would have another birthday, and was the old man of the group. Bobby claimed to be twenty-eight, according to Charles, but nobody knew for sure. If so, it was an old twenty-eight. He could have been forty. An old forty.

Bob and I talked as the miles rolled by. Plains radio was really bad, but he had his cassette player with him. Not only did he like big-band jazz, as do I, but he had a weakness for Firesign Theatre. As soon as we hit I-94 east, he put on their venerable "I Think We're All Bozos On This Bus." We listened for a few miles. I hadn't heard this in a while, so I thought I'd make an occasion of it.

"Bob, what if I roll a joint?"

"I don't know if I want to smoke, but you can. I've got a cold." I rolled a pinwheel joint, one of those real skinny ones, like a holdover from the Bebop days. ("Hey, Krupa, how about a reefer?")

I fired up. Bob couldn't resist. "Lemme have some of that."

As we smoked, we told about our lives and music backgrounds.

"You know," he said, "joining Bobby Love was a career move for me. I was on the road for two years, with the Tommy Riggs Show, and I figured it was time to change."

Riggs had been to Louisiana, Arkansas and Vegas. Tommy Riggs kept his family in Little Rock, Arkansas, and kept his show on the road about nine months a year. It seemed Bob had a good time with Riggs' show. On the road, no responsibilities, just work, coke and dames. Still, something was nagging him. He was concerned with the idea of "quality." Quality of art, of music, of life. To Bob, the concept had been succinctly explained in the book "Zen and the Art of Motorcycle Maintenance." I hadn't read the book, but that search for quality was what led me to join Bobby Love.

It also turned out that he had gone to Oak Park High School in Kansas City. So I had to ask him about a news story I'd heard a few years before. Some kid from Oak Park had started up a bulldozer, parked on the school grounds for a construction project, and drove it through the front door of the school building and down the hall. Yes, it was someone in Bob's class.

A few miles after we finished the joint, I saw something that made me wonder.

"Bob, look!" I pointed to the left, out of his side window. By the time he looked it had just disappeared behind a hill, like in the movies.

"What was it?" he asked. No trees, but plenty of glacier-scrubbed hills in North Dakota.

"Just wait a minute, it'll come out from behind that hill," I said, pointing.

It did.

"Holy shit!" he exclaimed. "You weren't kidding!" It was a thirty-foot buffalo that looked like papier maché but was probably made out of concrete. Some prairie prankster had stuck it out there for our edification and enjoyment. At least I knew I wasn't seeing things.

The ride home was more punishing than the drive up. Almost twenty-four hours of cold, rain, and even snow at one place in North Dakota. In case the truck and trailer, or even the van, for that matter, had a breakdown, we kept the caravan formation. This meant the same slow pace as going up, but it seemed worse.

In St. Joe, I got back in the camper with Charles, Bobby and Hollywood. Bob and Barry were almost home but the rest of us still had miles to go before we slept.

When I got home at two a.m. Monday, it was chilly and a dense, pea soup fog shrouded the city. It was almost too foggy to see. I took my bass and suitcase, leaving the other equipment with Bobby and Hollywood in the trailer, and they drove off to take Charles home. We were all exhausted. In less than two days we would be in Chillicothe, Missouri.

I didn't know whether to laugh or cry, but I was glad to be out of that damned camper.

He Don't Look Like Elvis

Chillicothe

THAT FIRST "WEEKEND" BACK home was rough. I was almost too wasted to move, and a little disoriented. Anne was glad to see me, but there was certainly no big reception. Numbly, I just lounged around the house.

It was a short rest. Tuesday, Bob picked me up in his van around twelve-thirty. Anne had stayed home from work to see me off. Barry was already with Bob, and then we went to pick up Charles. Also in the van were the Rhodes piano and speakers, the Crumar, Barry's amp and guitar, my bass, and, of course, all our luggage. In the event of a sudden stop, we would have been crushed. On the way out of town, we stopped to get some dope from one of my friends. We were now officially on the road, all in good spirits. We got on I-35 north.

"So," said Charles, sounding skeptical of the town's existence, "where is this Chillicothe?" Riding shotgun in the van, he scanned the road atlas. "Ah! Here it is. Not more than two hours' drive. You know how to go Bob?"

"More or less. Tell me where to get off the freeway." Then, "Barry! Where's that joint?" Barry and I were sitting on pillows behind Bob and Charles, passing it between us. Every now and then we would stand on our knees to hand it to Bob, and look out the window. The scenery wasn't real exciting along I-35 north, and not much improved along U.S. Highway 36, though more rural. It was a sunny day, and much warmer than North Dakota. Almost hot.

"Charles, when was Bobby gonna leave?" asked Barry.

"Sometime this afternoon. He and Hollywood are bringing the trailer up." We – the Love Machine – had decided that it was impractical and dangerous for more than two to ride in the truck. That way nobody had to be in the camper. We reasoned that, since Lee had lent Bobby the use of it, and they seemed to be good friends, and since Hollywood had to help Bobby with his wardrobe and stuff anyway, they got the truck. The rest of us rode in the van. There's that de facto division again.

We made it to Chillicothe, or Chili-con-carne, as Barry called it, about three p.m., got off the highway and turned left onto Highway 65, the main road through town. Right away we saw our motel on the west side of the road, made a mental note, and continued on to find the Duke's. Bobby had given us the address. Duke's was on Denver.

Not far from the motel we saw a Denver on our right, but it was only a narrow gravel road, lined on both sides by tall ragweed and a few trees. Bob slowed down for a look.

"Oh man, this can't be it." We agreed. He drove on. We passed a Sonic, which we duly noted for future use. Might be the best restaurant in town. We passed a Caterpillar tractor sales building that had a HUGE fake bulldozer on the roof. That would certainly prove to be a landmark. It was close to the Sonic. We passed through the town square. Eventually, we came to the north end of town. On our right was a large supermarket, "Open 24 Hours." Duly noted, for sure. On through the traffic light. It was open country again.

"Well, gentlemen," deadpanned Barry, "we seem to have run out of town."

"Lord, I guess!" said Bob. "There's only one thing to do." He hung a U-turn and headed back into town. Across from the supermarket we'd just seen was a gas station. Bob pulled in and Charles hopped out to ask directions. Followed to the letter, the instructions led us back to that same gravel road – Denver.

Duke's was a mile or so down the road, sitting at a T intersection with another gravel road. Aside from an electrical power booster station across the way, we were smack in the middle of a soybean field. We pulled into Duke's gravel parking lot, and stepped out of the van just as our dust cloud caught up with us. Nothing like a good stretch and a whiff of country air.

Duke's was a large, rectangular building with a western-style front, kind of like an old saloon, but without the swinging doors. It was relatively clean inside, but less roomy than it looked from the outside.

Rather than wait for Hollywood and Bobby – there was no way of knowing when they would arrive – we decided to unload the van and set up what we could. Just as we were about done unloading the van, Hollywood pulled in with the trailer. Bobby was back at the motel. Hollywood pitched in and we were set up in about an hour. We even did a sound check. Then we all headed back to the motel.

The elderly couple that ran the motel were friendly enough. They didn't flinch when Charles asked which way was north. Both pointed to it. The rooms were well kept, not too tacky – standard neutral blue, white trim. And the toilet seats had the official paper seal.

Seemingly, just another week in another town. I, however, had reason to be excited: I had friends in Chillicothe.

Clayton and Jana. Clayton had been the soundman for Woodland Green, the band I was in before Foxfire and the Love Machine. JT, our lead guitarist, had seen Clayton's ad in the Sunday paper and called him. That was that. We got to be good friends. Anne and Jana were really close.

Eventually, after Woodland Green died a death, Clayton got a job as engineer for a radio station in Tarkio, Missouri. After a couple of years he moved to the Chillicothe radio station. Anne and I hadn't seen Clayton and Jana since they lived in Tarkio.

As soon as I was situated in the motel room, I called and

talked to Jana. It was good to hear her voice. She said she would have Clayton come by the motel after work and pick me up for dinner, about five-thirty or six.

Jana and Clayton had a big old house not far from the square, in a neighborhood combining Victorian and rural post-Victorian architecture. Quiet. It was nice to have a home-cooked meal before opening night's show. I thought of Anne, who was coming up later in the week. This would be fun for us.

Clayton got me back to the motel in time to ride over to Duke's with the rest of the band. Duke, who, naturally, ran Duke's, had placed ads in the paper and had spots on the radio announcing the coming of Bobby Love. "Direct from Las Vegas!" Clayton and I had a good laugh over the radio spots. "Direct from Minot!"

But they worked. The place was crowded, especially by Tuesday night standards. Everyone was curious, looking to catch that old Elvis fever of yore. Even if by proxy.

The band did well on our dance set before the first show. It was good to see people dance, which they did precious little of in Minot, even though everyone there told us how much they liked the act. By the end of the first show, the crowd was hooked. Bobby, in his pink and black tux, was in fine form. During the second dance set, the audience really heated up.

"Gee, it's sure nice to see people who aren't afraid to dance," said Bob, doing some of his between-song patter. "Yeah, it's nice to see some hootin' and hollerin'. We just got back from a week in Minot, North Dakota, and those people don't dance."

At the words "Minot, North Dakota," a murmur moved through the crowd like wind in a wheat field. Snatches of "Minot . . . what? . . . Vegas?" reached the stage. Bob was baffled for a second. Then it hit him: the ads.

"Oops," he giggled into the mike, "did I say something wrong?" He looked around at us. We all had that "uh-oh" look. More giggles. Charles took control and kicked off a song. If it really bothered the audience, they didn't let on.

However, after the second show, where Bobby introduced the band and told where we're from, a woman cornered me.

"You're not really from Newport News, are you."

"Sure!" I said, laughing, playing the part.

"Aw, come on! You're not!" She was smiling slyly.

"I swear," I said solemnly, but she was having none of it. We both laughed, and I told her the story.

By the way, she wasn't from Chillicothe, either.

For someone who had gone to bed at three-thirty a.m., I woke up pretty early. About nine-thirty. Strange bed in a strange town. I'd taken Jana and Clayton up on their offer to let me stay with them while in Chillicothe. Not only, then, could I visit with old friends, but Charles could have the motel room to himself.

I got up, showered, dressed, and went downstairs.

"Good morning!" Jana greeted as I ambled into the kitchen. "Did you sleep well?"

I sat at the table. "Oh yes. How are you this morning?"

"I feel good. Clayton got off to work OK this morning. He had to go in early, so he was grouchy. As you can see, I'm just busy being domestic."

Indeed. The washing machine was going, the stove was going, and Jana was making some baby food for Phoebe, their daughter.

"You want some coffee?" she asked, in the middle of mashing peas.

"Point the way," I said, getting up to help myself.

"Cups are over there on the wall, and there's some honey on the counter. We don't use any sugar – is that all right?" she said, grinning. "When I get Phoebe fed, I'll make us some breakfast." I fixed my coffee and sat back at the table.

The sun was shining, and birds chirped with the cheerfulness of mid-May. There was none of the chill of Minot. Something about mornings out in the country. Always more clear and fresh. I sat silently for a while, drinking my coffee, while taking in the new surroundings. Jana sat down to feed Phoebe, who was in her high chair kicking happily.

"Here you go, Baby!" Like most babies, Phoebe got more food on her than in her. Especially stuff she didn't like. Carrots were OK, but mashed peas were out. At eighteen months, she knew what was what. She wasn't fond of oatmeal, either, but it was real good to spread on her face.

"Phoebe!" protested Jana, wiping her off. Phoebe yelled and laughed. Jana looked at me, and we both laughed too.

The kitchen was cluttered and homey. A lot of baby things and toys on the floor. How strange to be so far from home, and so nice to have friends there. I looked out the window and listened as Jana talked to Phoebe, her voice melodious in the morning, mingling with the birds. When Phoebe finished eating, Jana put her in her walker to play.

"Ready to eat?" Jana asked me.

"Let's have it."

"How about eggs and bacon with toast?"

"Boy, an American breakfast." We laughed, knowing we both tried to eat whole foods as much as possible. Ah, the granola years. So, bacon and eggs? Jana could tell that I was a little surprised.

"Well," she said, mocko serioso, "nobody's perfect."

Usually, I didn't eat much for breakfast. Toast, usually. But it was close enough to noon, almost eleven. Why not. I wouldn't get to eat again until dinner, probably, since the band was going to rehearse that afternoon. We were trying some new dance material.

It was a tasty breakfast, with a side bowl of oatmeal, although I don't wear it well. The cooking smell lingered while I helped Jana with the dishes.

"You don't have to do that," she mildly protested.
"Might as well make myself useful," I said.
"Clayton never helps with the dishes..."
Dishes done, we sat down to more coffee.
"Wait here!" I said suddenly. I dashed upstairs to my room, and was back in a few minutes.
"All right!" said Jana, as I lit a reefer. The dense, sweet aroma filled the kitchen while we silently savored each toke.

A warm stillness gradually permeated the room and seemed to seep outside where even the birds in the trees and bushes near the house sang a more languid tune. From my recent years as a surveyor, and high school years hunting and hiking, I had learned to identify some bird songs. There was the fine "tcheew-tcheew" of a cardinal, the raspy "aahnt-aahnk" of a blue jay, and the full-third (musically speaking) "he-ho" of the meadow lark, with some assorted mourning doves and others for good measure. A nice chorus. Not to mention some chirping crickets.

Jana looked over across the table, and I felt her eyes as I stared out the back door. I turned to meet them.

"Well, Frank, you've come a long way from Woodland Green. What do you think?"

"It's weird, Jana. All that time we struggled with that band, only to get nowhere. Not even many gigs. And that JT was so bullheaded!"

And I do mean bullheaded. Or I should say, goat-headed, since he's a Capricorn. Once, on a hot summer day, JT, Donny, a non-musician friend, and I pulled in at the Dairy Queen on Independence Avenue for a hot fudge sundae or something. This particular DQ was walk-up only – no inside seating. Donny and I were going to eat right there, in my car. Why wait? It would all melt before we got back to the house, and anyway I couldn't hold the sundae and drive a stick too. For some reason, JT refused to eat in the car. I told him I didn't mind him eating in my car, but that didn't seem to be the problem.

"Go ahead and eat before your sundae melts." Innocent enough. But nothing doing. JT sat in the back seat and fumed while Donny and I ate ours, and took our time about it.

"JT!" she hooted. "I just can't believe that guy. He was a good guitar player . . ."

"Yeah, but such a prick," I finished. "I'd have never had anything to do with him, except he was good. But what a pain to work with." And, for all that, I did actually like the guy.

"Have you seen him lately?"

"No, not for a long time."

JT and I had met while attending different high schools together. Actually, I was in high school, he had dropped out to play guitar. I joined his band after a friend introduced us. Although we sometimes seemed at odds, for some reason we became friends. Being out of school would eventually leave JT vulnerable to the draft, so he joined the Army at seventeen. He was sent to Viet Nam, came back in one piece but not the same.

"Bands," I mused. "Sometimes I think I should know better by now. But I don't know . . ."

"What do you think of this band?" asked Jana.

"Well, it's a good one, and I like the members. All of us get along and we play together well."

"What do you think will happen?"

"I don't know," I said, shaking my head. "I like playing, but you could play in bars the rest of your life and still not get anywhere. No vacation or sick leave. No home. But on the other hand, what job is really secure? We're all going to die in the end." I wasn't being gloomy, just matter-of-fact. "So why not do what you feel?"

"I know, Frank." Jana's voice was soothing. "It's crazy, isn't it? Sometimes I wonder just what I'm doing here. With a baby! I wanted to have a baby so badly, and now, sometimes, I just don't know. Clayton is having a hard time adjusting. Maybe I forced it on him. What'll we do if we split up? Every now and then, I just feel lost."

We thought a minute. Jana spoke again.

"How does Anne feel about all this?"

"She's the one who got me into it, so to speak." I told her the tale about the Hot List. "And the rest is history," I said.

"And here you are."

"And here I am." I moved to put the mood in the upswing. "I certainly intend to make the best of it. At least, I don't have to survey any more. For a while. If ever."

"Would you ever go back to your old job?"

"Damn. Not if I can help it. But who knows what will happen?"

"Do you like being on the road?" Jana wasn't really grilling me. I was glad to have someone to talk with about it. Someone who had been through some of the same things and saw them from the other side. She knew who I was.

Like I knew Jana. She would come over with Clayton to practice at my place, where I lived with Anne, JT and Mark, the sax and rhythm guitar player. Hanging out while we practiced, Jana and Anne became friends. I really liked Jana.

"On the road . . ." I mused. "Well, I tell you. It's hard. To be away from home like that . . . When I got home from Minot, it was bizarre. I was a little disoriented. Strange to relate to being home again, good to be home, but different because we'd been on our own, Anne and I. Just as I was getting used to being back, we're on the road again. Now what the hell kind of deal is that? Besides, Anne has to work in the day, so I don't get to see her until the evening. It's disorienting."

Jana nodded emphatically. "I know what you mean. Clayton went on the road some when he was soundman with Colt .45. It was weird at first. Sleeping alone and all that. But I think it made me look at myself, and I got stronger. It was exciting to discover that I could function on my own. But it was disorienting, as you said."

"Yeah, bands are hard on relationships." I was staring into my cup.

Basta! Enough!

I lightened up and looked at Jana. "How do you like it here? Is it better than Tarkio?"

Jana sighed. "Oh, definitely better than Tarkio. That station was such a wreck! Everybody bailed out. This is a bigger town, too. There's still not too much to do, though. Not that I can do much with Phoebe, but, you know, I guess sometimes I'd like to move back to the city."

I nodded. I told her of some goofy anecdotes from my earlier band days, like the time at Northeast High School's Teen Town, when I backhanded John Hook, who kept trying to grab my mike to sing. He wanted to impress his pals, and when I smacked him they started to rush me. Our bass player, Stan, stepped up front with his bass while I fixed bayonets with my guitar's whammy bar. Between us, we pushed them back and shoved them away, avoiding a rumble. Jana talked about when Clayton was doing sound with Colt .45, and how it was so boring and lonely for her when he was on the road. She asked when Anne was coming up.

"I think tomorrow, Thursday. She plans to leave Friday, and tonight she's going to call."

"It'll be nice to see her," Jana said.

As if on cue, we stood up and moved to the front room where Jana rolled another joint. I called Bob at the motel to find out about practice. He would be by around one-thirty, he said.

It never ceased to amaze us – the Love Machine and Hollywood – how people reacted to Bobby's show.

Especially women.

"I think it's a hoot," said Jana after seeing the show. "I

know it's phony and it turns me on!"

"Close your eyes . . . you'll swear it's Elvis when you know it isn't!" So it said on the flyers.

It wasn't entirely misleading, judging by the screaming and cheering. In fact, to us it often seemed that people treated the arrival of Bobby's show as something akin to the Second Coming. Yes, Elvis was dead, but nobody wanted to let him go.

Men liked the show too, but there was also a good dose of jealousy because "their" women were screaming for Bobby. He certainly reveled in the attention they showered on him. Women mobbed him for scarves, and crowded the dressing room between and after a show to get autographs and kisses. He never turned them away. "I like 'em all," he would say. "Eight to eighty, blind, crippled, or crazy."

And for only four dollars, they could buy an eight-by-ten color glossy of Bobby in action. This last item really cracked us up.

"Boy," quipped Barry, after looking over Hollywood's stack of framed photos, "I still think he looks like Judy Garland."

On Thursday Anne had come up to Chillicothe to visit Jana and Clayton. That night they were in the audience. It was nice to have some moral support. After our dance set, Barry, Bob, and I stepped outside for fresh air. Inside, the crowded club was foggy with cigarette smoke and loud with people talking. Just before we got to the door, we overheard a guy talking to his friends. "Aw shit, he don't look like Elvis."

The three of us were laughing about it as we stood outside in the parking lot, passing a joint. We watched a man come out and go to his car, carrying one of the nefarious pictures. He put it in the car. On the way back, he stopped and chatted with us for a minute. Although in good spirits, he was a little incredulous. "Jeez! Four bucks for a picture of a guy that ain't even Elvis!" His wife, or girlfriend, had gotten to him. He laughed good-naturedly and went back inside.

Bob went to get ready for the next set while Barry and I finished the joint. It was nearly time for the second show.

Bobby was sitting in the dressing room – Duke's office – finishing a joint of his own. He was already dressed for the second show, Elvis in Vegas. Tonight, he wore the dark-blue jumpsuit.

Hollywood was organizing scarves to put on stage for Bobby to give away. Those scarves were a real draw. Charles was standing in front of the mirror on the closet door, adjusting his vest.

Barry and I came in from outside and passed through the bar, dodging through the crowd toward the dressing room. Bob was on stage warming up his Rhodes. A few women were still huddled around the dressing room door. Bobby had cleared them out of the room so he could change costumes. Not that he was modest, but it helped the mystique.

"Excuse me," said Barry, elbowing through the crush. We slipped into the dressing room. A couple of women caught sight of Bobby, and I had to fend them off as I closed the door.

"Back! Back!"

"Stick around for the show, Baby!" teased Bobby as the door shut. "Heh-heh." He took a swig of beer. Already, Duke's office was paved with beer cans and bottles. Every available flat surface was covered.

"Hey, it's the band!" greeted Hollywood.

"Holywooooood!" called Barry and I in unison.

"All right, guys," said Charles, feigning disgust. "You done smokin' your dope so we can play?"

"You tell 'em, Charles," crowed Bobby, hitting off a roach. "OK, guys, remember, tonight we'll do "Kentucky Rain" after "American Trilogy." Looks like a pretty good crowd out there." Bobby was happy and ready to roll.

Details, primping, details. Bobby finished putting on his

makeup, Barry and I prepared ourselves, straightening our shirts and vests, just as Bob stepped back into the dressing room.

"Hey, y'all, got a good bunch of 'em out there tonight. Let's go knock some dicks in the dirt!"

"Yeah, man!" "Right arm!" deadpanned Hollywood and Barry.

Bob sniffed the air. "You guys been smokin' dope! Where is it?"

"Aw, man, you missed it!" said Bobby. "Heh-heh."

"Well, shit." He found a handy roach on an empty beer can and burned it. "That's better."

Hollywood took the scarves out to the stage and set them up for Bobby, and then manned the spotlight.

In single file, team Love Machine walked out of the dressing room and took the stage. Bobby waited in the dressing room.

The audience hushed at the first strains of "2001." As the music level rose, Hollywood brought up the spotlight like a sunrise. Excitement hung in the air, draped over the tables.

A wave of screams swept the women as Bobby hit the spotlight to the intro of "Viva Las Vegas."

Thursday's show was a smash. We were working up to Friday and the weekend. It would be great. All of us in the troupe were feeling good about the show. The band was tightening up all the time, learning new songs for the dance sets. The Love Machine was coming into its own.

After the show that night, Anne and I went back to Clayton and Jana's. They invited the Love Machine and Hollywood over to their house to hang out with some of their other friends. We were all thankful for the hospitality. It was a nice break in the routine and fun meeting new people. We all talked, drank and smoked into the wee hours.

By late Friday afternoon, Anne had gone back to Kansas City, and I was left to my own devices. Clayton drove me around Chillicothe to see the sights, such as they were, during which we smoked dope, talked over old stories and new details.

Before our arrival in Chillicothe, Bobby and Duke had put out a tremendous amount of hype, taking out newspaper ads, buying radio spots – "Live, from Las Vegas!" Lee Miller was there ahead of us too. He handled the details, ran interference, and helped get things ready for "Elvis Week," creating a stir before Bobby landed.

Clayton was asking me about the future of the Bobby Love Show, when he dropped the bomb.

"When are you guys going to Japan?"

I choked on a toke. "Where the hell did you hear that?"

"Well, we had Bobby's front man – whatsisname – Lee? I interviewed him on the radio show today. He was telling us about this big tour he's got planned for Bobby – Hawaii, Japan."

"Fuck," I snorted, "we'll be lucky to get out of the state! Back home, even! Japan, my ass! That Lee Miller . . ."

I caught my breath.

"You know where he got that? Remember Lee Waterman?" Lee had been the drummer in Woodland Green. My oldest friend, half Japanese, born in Tokyo.

Clayton's eyebrows rose. "Sure. You and Lee could smoke more dope than anyone I knew in the Free World."

"Well," I continued, "it's all my fault. Lee has a cousin in Japan – Junshon. He was visiting during the time that I started with Bobby. Junshon owns a nightclub in Yokohama, called Fridays, and he loves American music. He has a lot of money. A lot of money. One time when he was visiting, he told Lee to buy him a car and ship it to Japan. He had the money in his pocket. Literally, pocket change. Anyhow, I hinted to Bobby that if we could get to Japan, we could play at Junshon's club. What did I know? I thought the show was movin'. We're good! But we can barely make it to Chillicothe. How the fuck is Bobby going to get to Japan? Swim? There's an image: Bobby swimming in his Elvis suit. Sharks!"

All of us in the band thought the show would be a hit in Japan. And I know Junshon would have loved to have us there. But we also knew we'd never get there unless things drastically changed.

"Nonetheless," I concluded, "we still gotta play Duke's."

Duke's was jumping that night.

People were standing in places where we didn't know there were places. Duke sold a lot of steaks and potatoes, but the crowd was hungry for more than that. It was a far cry from Tuesday night when, during a quiet part of "Suspicious Minds," Duke had turned on the blender to make a margarita.

The Love Machine eyed the audience from the stage. From time to time we glanced at each other. I looked at Charles, and he grinned back. Was this real? We had to laugh.

But we also had to pay attention to Bobby's cues. That was the thing that made the show float. As the band became more and more of a working unit, it became easier to follow Bobby into whatever alien territory he might wander.

Extend a chorus? Sure. Bring down the volume and vamp while Bobby talked, or gave out scarves? No problem. The more we worked together, the easier it was to work from feeling, rather than just playing by rote.

Still, no matter how much we stood back and looked at the scene, we couldn't escape the fact that we were a very real part of it. Without the Love Machine, there could be no Bobby Love. And as much as we laughed about it, it was exciting.

Somehow, we managed to create that excitement, enough for the audience to suspend disbelief. At times, I found myself wondering, is this what it was like to be Elvis? Is this what the Beatles talked about? Kesey too? It's that palpable energy that moves in waves through an audience.

That kind of magic? In a bar in Chillicothe, Missouri? Maybe, in some small way.

Bobby could do no wrong that night. I knew it was out of control when the first fumes of a joint wafted up out of the audience near the bandstand. Dope at Duke's!

Saturday was closing night. We would spend one more night in the motel, and hit the road Sunday morning. We were heading to Atchison – again! – to do a Mother's Day Concert that Sunday evening.

Everyone expected that it would be even wilder than the Friday show. All indications were "go." Duke's was full that night – standing room only – but not packed. There was sort of an anticlimactic air. Still, the crowd was humming.

The first show was a great success. Our dance set went well also. Afterward, we sat in the dressing room getting ready for the second show. The last show. Bobby was sitting behind Duke's desk, feet up, stoking a reefer, putting the ashes in one of the many beer cans he had strewn around the office, er, dressing room.

"Bobby," teased Bob, "I thought you liked to do your show straight!"

"Well, yeah," he said. "I like to do the first show straight. But for the second show, I drop a red, smoke a joint, and I ain't afraid a nuthin'. Heh-heh." We paraded out and took the stage.

It was a solid show. "Viva Las Vegas." "Suspicious Minds." The hits kept rolling and the crowd was ecstatic. But, somehow it lacked the wildness of Friday. Maybe there had been a certain element of danger, I guess.

Then we got to "Hurt." It was a favorite of the crowds, and a real showcase for Bobby's voice. Quite dramatic, it begins with a tense rolling of bass and drums, then a wailing "I-I-I-IIII'mmm – Sooo – Hu-urt." The lights were low, and Charles and I went into the intro. Bobby went into his stance, and cut loose.

A strangled "AWWWK!" escaped his throat.

Of course, Bobby was mortified, and we were stunned. Surely it would break the illusion. The crowd took it well, though some snickered and laughed. But they didn't leave.

We cracked up without openly laughing. Even so, we didn't stop playing the intro. Never missed a beat. Roll-roll-roll-roll . . .

It was bizarre. Even Bobby laughed, although he was blushing through his makeup. We were surprised. Bobby had never slipped up that badly before.

But we didn't lose a beat. At first, we thought that Bobby would quickly recover. Instead, he hung his head. Looked at the floor. Looked at the audience.

Barry looked at Bob. I looked at Charles. Charles looked at Barry. Somehow, we all looked at each other at once. Still, we didn't miss a beat. Without speaking, we agreed. Don't stop. Truly, the only thing worse than making a mistake during a performance is stopping after it.

Bobby glared at us. At Bob, in particular. He had that "aren't you guys going to stop?" look. "No," we looked back. What else could we do? Besides, we were too far into it to stop by that time.

There was nothing for Bobby to do but sing.

This time he hit it right. The crowd loved it.

Jana and Clayton met me after the show to say good-bye. We all hugged. I then joined the others in packing up the show. Striking the set. We could tear down and load in an hour.

Barry and I stopped to get a drink from the bar. As Joanne, the bartender, brought our drinks, Barry commented on the smaller crowd.

Joanne chuckled. "I think Duke did that to himself," she said. "He put those ads in the paper saying the show was sold out, and that kept people away. He's gonna have to eat a lot of baked potatoes."

In a short while, we were back at the motel. Charles and I were just settling into TV when Hollywood came by and said Bobby wanted everybody to come to his room. Hollywood didn't know why. It sounded like a meeting. Charles and I took our time.

Hollywood had just gotten out of the shower when we arrived. Bobby was sitting cross-legged on his bed. Barry was there already, and watching TV.

"Where's Bob?" asked Charles.

"He'll be here soon," said Barry.

Bobby paid Charles and me.

"Anyone for popcorn?" asked Hollywood, filling his popper. As the kernels jumped, he lit a joint and passed it around.

Whatever Bobby had on his mind, it would wait for Bob. We ate popcorn and smoked, watched TV. Made small talk with Hollywood. Bobby was unusually quiet. In about twenty minutes, Bob showed up.

Bobby got right to it. He said he wasn't satisfied with how things were going: The show wasn't tight enough. There was not enough new material. The dance sets weren't exciting.

This caught us off guard, considering how the week had gone. But we dutifully kicked around ideas for improvement, told Bobby where we thought he was right or wrong.

Our main gripe was bookings. Lee Miller seemed to be working against us. Wednesday, outside of Duke's during our break, we ran into Dave, who worked for Jerry Plantz, Bobby's agent. He had come to see how things were going. I'd never met Dave but Bob knew him. Dave said Lee lost us several jobs that Jerry had booked for us. And those were just the gigs he knew about. The pattern looked like this: Jerry would book us into a club, and then Lee, as advance man, would go check the place out. Invariably, he would argue about money, demand more than what the contract specified, and the job would be canceled. Very frustrating. We were afraid of being condemned to Genova's forever.

Bobby was more frustrated than coherent. He had gotten more loaded since the show. More drinking. More reds. More wired. He didn't take much stock in our ideas, and acted irritated. At times, the air was a little tense. Bobby wanted somebody besides himself and Lee to blame. We were genuinely interested in improving the show, but didn't know exactly what Bobby wanted or expected.

Bob, on the other hand, was outspoken. As leader of the band, he felt responsible for success or failure. It was that quality thing. It was his contention that as far as material for the show went, he was following Bobby's orders.

Which was true. Bobby gave us a little freedom to choose songs for the dance set, but he wanted a certain style. No stuff along the lines of Elvis, or any rockabilly material. To Barry, this made the least sense. A band that played some good old rockabilly tunes along with jumpin' rhythm and blues would be the perfect supporting act for the show. The styles made a perfect tie-in. But disco was hot, and Bobby nixed it. His heart was set on the current disco sort of stuff. We couldn't really argue about it. We just honestly told him what we thought. After all, it was Bobby's show. However, within this guideline, we managed to come up with some fairly hot tunes to showcase our talents, disco and rockabilly notwithstanding. In the end, Bobby admitted that we really weren't all that bad. Quite kickass, actually.

At the heart of it, I think, was the fact that he was still hurting over the Hurt incident earlier that night. But that never came up.

Anyhow, we managed to bring the discussion to what seemed like an amicable end. Bob was the first to get up to leave, disgusted with the hazy pointlessness of it all. He was just about to open the door when Bobby asked him if he could use his tape player to listen to the tape of the night's performance.

For some reason, this really rubbed Bob the wrong way and was the last straw.

"You mean, Bobby, that you can sit there and complain about our work, and give us a load of shit, and then turn around and want to borrow my player?"

"Well, yeah . . ."

"I'm tired of it. Why don't you get your own? I had to buy a van so I could haul my equipment around the country without being killed, and do things to support this show, and what do you do? Give us shit!"

In a flash, Bobby leaped off the bed, landed in front of Bob, grabbed him by the lapels of his jacket, picked him up and threw him on the bed flat on his back, jumped up on the bed himself, sat on Bob's chest and raised his fist.

Bobby froze. He didn't hit Bob. I think it sank in what was happening. The rest of us sat silent, thunderstruck. It had happened so fast, no one had time to react. We all looked at each other.

Bob looked over at us. "Hey! Help me out here!"

We all yelled at Bobby to get off, but he was still frozen. We all looked at each other again. I was pretty sure what Charles, Barry and I would do if Bobby moved to hit Bob. But I wasn't sure about Hollywood, who was as dumbfounded as the rest of us.

Again, we all yelled at Bobby. He slumped, limp like a rag doll, got up, and helped Bob to his feet, sincerely apologizing. Bob shook his head and left.

We all cleared out after that, going back to our rooms. Charles and I didn't talk about it, except to wonder what the hell we were doing there.

Next morning, we checked out of the motel. The tension of the previous night was gone, although we were all a little wary of Bobby. Nothing, however, was said. Bobby seemed in a much better mood. As Charles and I were going out to Bob's van, I happened to get a glimpse through the open door of Hollywood and Bobby's room. They were just packing up to leave. There were enough empty beer cans and bottles to cover every surface, and enough roaches to make a dime bag, just like at Duke's. I waved at them as I passed. Poor maids, I thought, seeing the carnage.

Bobby and Hollywood were heading on to Atchison. The rest of us decided to eat first, and stopped at a local barbecue. Charles brought in his tape player, so we could hear some new songs to learn. The owners, or whoever it was behind the counter, told him to turn it off. We ate and split. Good-bye, Chillicothe!

"God," said Barry as we cruised down Highway 36. "I can't believe we're going back to Atchison."

"I know," said Bob. "How many people are going to see Bobby Love on Mother's Day?"

The concert was at the National Guard armory auditorium, not the Melrose. Bobby had arranged for motel rooms in Atchison, and these weren't at the Melrose, either. About three that afternoon, we pulled into town, found the motel and Bobby, and went to set up for the show.

The armory turned out to be a neat old building. The stage was a real stage, with plenty of room, curtains and lighting, but the best part was backstage. Behind the curtains, and in the wings, were all sorts of old vaudeville posters. Originals! If only I could have taken one home. They were mounted on the walls and on boards too big to sneak out. We set up the equipment, then we went back to the motel to clean up.

The motel was modest but clean. Much better than the Melrose, and we had water. Barry speculated how long it would take Bobby to trash his room. He'd have to work fast, since we were leaving that night.

Now it was time to eat.

"Charles, what should we eat?" asked Bob.

"I want something good!" I piped up. To me, that meant steaks, Chinese food, tacos.

"Ha! Good luck!" quipped Bob.

In Atchison, we were faced with a bewildering array of choices. There was Shoney's Big Boy; McDonald's, of course; Taco Bell; and Pizza Hut. Alas, no Long John Silver's.

"What do you think, Charles? Your choice," said Bob.

"Pizza."

"So be it."

"Sounds like the healthiest thing here," I said resignedly.

"How about 'EAT'?" jibed Barry.

"Hey, Slick, wanna be introduced? Huh, sumbich?" dramatized Bob. We laughed.

So putt-putt, to the Pizza Hut. And we made sure not to put any pork on Charles' half of the pizza. No sausage or pepperoni. Like Charles always said: "Lips that touch swine, will never touch mine."

"Your what?" we always asked.

After dinner, it was time to rock and roll.

Through the wonder of daylight saving time, it was still light for the seven o'clock show. Late sun poured through the auditorium windows, so we helped Hollywood pull down the shades to darken the hall as best we could to make the spotlight look brighter. He had put the light on the upper side bleachers, to our left. It was a good setup. Usually, Hollywood had to make do setting the light on two bar tables pushed together. Not only could the tables wobble, there was always the dangerous prospect of a careening drunk knocking him off. The spotlight used a lot of juice and got really hot.

The dressing room this time was large and, in contrast to the age of the building, had been modernized with carpeting and new paint. It was the real thing, not just a repurposed broom closet. Connie, president of the Bobby Love Fan Club, was sitting on the floor cutting out scarves for Bobby to give away. There were piles of polyester material, light blue, red, yellow, white and more, all over the floor.

When Bobby was ready, the Love Machine went out to the stage, and took our places behind the closed curtain. We could hear the audience out in the auditorium. It didn't sound big.

"You wait," said Bob. "The curtain will open, and nobody will be there."

"Empty hall," chuckled Barry. "Lee Miller does it again."

For this show, the plan was to play a short dance set before Bobby's act.

We began playing one of our dance numbers and the curtain opened on maybe a hundred people, mostly preteen and teenage girls, with some boys. And some parents. The dance set really got 'em up out of their seats, having a good time. For a small crowd, they were lively. We played about twenty or thirty minutes, and the curtain closed. Expectation hung in the air.

After a short break, we were ready. It was Elvis time.

We began the 2001 theme and the curtain went up. Bobby took the stage to the strains of CC Rider. By the second song, the girls had crowded right up to the stage apron, screaming and clapping.

Bobby played right up to them. They loved it when he gave out scarves. No kisses, though. Every now and then, Bob would cast a look over to us. We all had the same thought: some irate father was going to come out of the audience and wale on Bobby, thinking he was being a little too fresh with his daughter.

But no. It was all good, clean fun for the girls and boys. It was strange to see people younger than the band members by half who were such Elvis fans. What was it? Did they get it from their parents? Maybe, but it was more than that. Surely it wasn't Bobby. No, something more primal was going on here. Maybe that combination of Elvis, Bobby, and rock 'n' roll. And the Love Machine.

After the show, we packed up and went back to the motel. I was looking forward to going home. So was Charles. We went over to Bob's room to see when he was leaving.

"Say, Bob," asked Charles, "can we ride back with you?"

Bob shuffled his feet a little. "Well, uh, I'm not going back tonight."

"I thought we were all going back tonight," I said.

"Well, I'm staying with Jane here tonight." He had that "What can I do?" look.

"Fuck," I said. "If I'd known, I could have made arrangements for Anne to be here." Charles and I looked at each other. We went outside to find Barry.

Barry's girlfriend, Debbie, had come with her sister to see the show, so Barry was riding back with them. With three people and Barry's equipment in the Volkswagen, there just wasn't any room. We went to Bobby. He was sitting in his room, talking to Lee Miller.

"Bobby," I began, "are you going back to Kansas City tonight?"

"Naw, I'm gonna stay here a couple of days with some friends."

"Well, what about Hollywood?"

"He's gonna stay, too. Don't you guys wanna stay?" He really seemed surprised, and maybe a little hurt.

"No, we thought we were going back tonight."

"Well, we were. But we had these motel rooms already, so we figured we might as well use 'em."

"Yeah, but Charles and I need to get home tonight." We didn't really need to, but did want to.

Bobby shrugged. "Call a taxi. Heh-heh."

I was pissed. "Aw man, this sucks. You should have told us. We could have made sure to have a ride. What about the truck?"

"Hollywood and I are gonna ride back in it. You can ride

back tomorrow or the next day, with us if you want. Whenever we leave."

I was on the verge of some serious abuse when Lee broke in. "Wait, wait. Take my car. Here . . ." He pulled the keys out of his pocket and handed them to me. "Just leave the keys under the hood when you get home. I'll be by to pick it up tomorrow sometime."

"Thanks, Lee," I said. Lee came through for us that time, for sure.

Charles and I packed the car in a hurry – all we had was our clothes and my bass. The equipment was all in the trailer. Two more days and we'd be back on the road. We pulled out of Atchison about midnight.

Lee's car was a 1970 Javelin, in about the same shape as the truck. Beat to hell. But, it ran. It was almost out of gas and, of course, there were no open stations in Atchison late Sunday night, Mother's Day. None on the highway, either. I was driving, and was careful not to have a heavy foot on the pedal. Nervously, I watched the gas needle and the road. "Jeez, I hope we don't have to push."

We got to the open road out of town, and the darkness closed in around us, except for the lighted instrument panel and the headlights.

"Well, Frank," Charles began, "what do you think?"

"I think this sucks."

"Me too, man. No communication."

"But what do you expect? Those guys don't have anybody in town to go home to. What do they care?"

"Yeah, I know."

"Sometimes I think, 'Why'd I leave my job for this?' We don't need this abuse, Charles. Goddamn . . ."

"I know. I keep thinking that it'll be all right. If we can keep the band together, maybe we can get a gig and leave Bobby. You know we're good and people like us . . ."

"That's why I joined in the first place," I said. "I knew we'd be a good band. But it's so hard to progress; like being lost in the shuffle or something."

"But I don't want to go back to my job," said Charles. "I'm determined to make a go of it this time. I've been working for this all my life. What else can I do?"

"I know what you mean. It kills me to think of going back. If I can keep from it, I won't. But sometimes I wonder what I ever saw in music. Sometimes I think I'd have been better off with no talent at all, and just be happy at a job. I mean, I had a good job, not cooped up in an office, outside, the whole city to work in. Why leave? Most people would have given their left arm to have a job like that, and I tried to get away."

"But Frank, don't you see? We're artists. We've got to play. What else can you do?"

"I know. It's worse than drug addiction. Lord knows I've tried to quit. But I keep coming back. If only something would come of it, I could feel better. A guy could grow old playing in bars and never have anything to show for it. No vacation, or sick leave." I was quiet a minute. "Well, I certainly don't have anything better happening at the moment, so I'm not quitting yet."

"Neither am I," asserted Charles. We stared out of the windshield, watching the yellow line on the road.

The gas held out, and finally I dropped Charles off at home. I got home about one-thirty a.m. I lugged my suitcase and bass inside, and went upstairs to the bedroom. Anne was asleep. When I learned that no one was coming home from Atchison, I had called home. No answer.

"Hi, honey," I said softly. Anne stirred slowly and looked up in the darkness. "Oh, you're home. Hi."

"How are you doing? It's good to be back."

"I'm OK, but let me sleep. I've got to work tomorrow." Not that I had expected a parade or anything, but I had struggled so hard to get home.

"OK," I said.

I undressed and went back downstairs to smoke a joint. What was happening? Here I'd finally gotten what I wanted: a working band. Now it seemed like a mirage.

Eventually, I went to bed.

I awoke about eleven the next morning, remembering that Anne had said good-bye when she went to work. Our friend Anita, who also worked at City Hall, picked her up so I could have the car that day. After a shower and coffee, I took my acoustic guitar and drove to Loose Park. No use staying inside on a sunny day, and getting pasty like Bobby Love. I hoped that by the time I got back, Lee's car would be gone. I and the other band members would be in touch to plan our next move.

Flier announcing the Bobby Love Show premier at the Monroe Inn, March 22, 1978

Bobby Love and the Love Machine
L-R: Bob, Frankie, Bobby, Barry, Charles
Photo: Barry Johnson

Photos

Bobby Love in Gold Lamé
Photo: Barry Johnson

Bobby Love on stage
Photo: Frank C. Siraguso

Bobby Love on stage
Photo: Frank C. Siraguso

He Don't Look Like Elvis

Bobby Love on stage
Photo: Frank C. Siraguso

Mother's Day Concert ticket,
May 14, 1978, Atchison, Kansas

Bobby Love Fan Club
application form table tent

Genova's ad in Marquee, April 11, 1978

Photos

L-R: Charles, Barry, Frankie, Bob
The Embers, Poplar Bluff, Missouri
Photo: Patsy Sylvester

Frankie Stone
The Embers, Poplar Bluff, Missouri
Photo: Patsy Sylvester

Barry Johnson
The Embers, Poplar Bluff, Missouri
Photo: Patsy Sylvester

Torch Light, Minot, North Dakota
Photo: Barry Johnson

Glasgow

THE PARK WAS GREAT. I could sit out in the sun and enjoy it, instead of having to work, like when I was a surveyor. I had a lot of ambivalence about that, though. True, it was nice not having to work out in the sun, allowing me just to enjoy it. But on the other hand, there was something purposeful about being out there surveying. We weren't merely loafing. In the long run, it felt good to be a working musician, and in my heart I felt I had done the right thing by joining the band. However it ended up.

Other people were out, too. What kind of jobs did they have? They couldn't all be musicians. There were so many folks out, it seemed like a holiday. But, it was only Monday, and just after one in the afternoon.

I found an open space on a sunny slope and got out the guitar. Since I played bass with the Love Machine, I rarely took time to just sit and play guitar. It wasn't practical to take it on the road. It would be too easy to steal and there was no time to play it. Also, playing every night, there just wasn't the inclination to play for fun. It was my work, even if it was fun sometimes, so off hours were spent otherwise. Lounging, reading.

But there was nobody to talk to. Anne still worked in the day, and she wouldn't be home until five-thirty or so. All my other friends worked, too. Except for the band members, of course. But I would see them soon enough. I felt adrift.

I played tunes and smoked a joint in the sun. Quite luxurious. By two-thirty, I had had enough sun, and so had my guitar. Home for lunch. I was relieved to see Lee had taken his car. I was really grateful he let us use it.

Bob called around four. We weren't going on the road, as it turned out. The gig, in Topeka, Kansas, had fallen through. He suspected Lee again, but wasn't positive. Instead, we were going to work at Genova's Chestnut Inn for the next two weeks.

Certainly, this had its advantages. For one thing, I would get to see Anne every day, such as it was. For another, it would give us a chance to eat at home, sleep in our own beds, and learn some new material. Of course, we continued to learn new tunes on the road, but we felt that this would give us some stability. Even musicians need that sometimes.

It was like old home week back at Genova's. We felt comfortable, even if it did have that shoot-your-way-in-and-out quality about it. Pete and Joe were there, as were the familiar waitresses. Everyone said hi and seemed glad to see us as we set up the equipment. We were even expecting to see some of the same faces in the crowd. There would be no disappointment on that count. Cindy and Roxy showed up, for several nights. Surprised at my own reaction, I was glad to see them!

The Genovas and their customers liked Bobby's show. Something out of the ordinary, not just another country band. For our part, we knew that these folks would respond better than anybody breathing in Minot. And, for all the legendary violence of the place, we still felt safe.

All things being equal, though, Genova's had a drawing appeal more limited than it had in past years, when all the name country acts were coming through. Times had changed. It was partly location. The old Northeast neighborhood had deteriorated and was not as hip as the Westport area had become. And it was partly Genova's well-earned reputation as a real shitkicking joint. Too bad. Those uptowners would have been safer than they thought. Not only that, the drinks were cheaper and the food better. So, in reality, it was now a local bar with an oddity floor show. In short, we couldn't set the town on fire playing at the Chestnut Inn. By the end of our second week, the crowds weren't so crowded. We were ready to hit the road again. At the end of the week, we found out our next job was in Glasgow.

No, not Glasgow, Scotland. Glasgow, Missouri.

On Saturday we closed at Genova's, and on Monday had to be in Glasgow. We would leave Monday afternoon. Not much of a weekend. Anne and I spent Sunday sitting around watching TV. We talked little. There wasn't much to say. Couldn't make any plans because I was leaving again. We just quietly, separately, hung out together.

Bob picked me up in the van just before noon. Charles and Barry were already with him. I packed my suitcase and bass in the van, leaped in, and we were on our way.

"Hey, Frank," greeted Charles cheerfully from the shotgun seat. "Are you ready?"

It was almost a relief to be back on the road. It sure beat hanging around the house waiting to go. Maybe I should have stayed that night in Atchison.

We all seemed ready to roll. As we zoomed onto I-70 east, Barry lit a joint. Of course, Charles grieved us about it. "There you guys go again, smokin' that dope." Undeterred, we toked on.

"Well," Bob informed us, "Glasgow is about two hours away. On the river."

Glasgow is a farming town, on the east side of the Missouri River, about mid-state. (It would be on the north side, but the river takes a turn and runs south about 20 miles.) It had been an important riverboat stop during the steamboat heyday of the mid-1800s. Must have been quite a town in Mark Twain's time.

The main drag is about three blocks long. There was a restaurant, post office, a feed store, and other small businesses. We also found a drugstore where we could get wonderful, old-fashioned chocolate sodas. It was truly a relic. Marble counter, wire-legged chairs, ceiling fans. Also, there was a pool hall, and there was one bar, Tommy's, where we would work.

It was a little after two-thirty when we pulled into town, finding Tommy's on the south end as we entered. Our motel was on the other side of town, just outside about a mile. It was at the bottom of a long, straight hill, surrounded by soybean fields. Across the road was a drive-in burger joint.

We decided that it's always best to check into the motel first whenever possible, just to make sure there's a place to stay. (And water, too!) The Skyview Motel. Not bad. Small, clean. We moved in to our rooms, Charles determined true north, and we headed back to town.

Hollywood and Bobby had already arrived at Tommy's when we got back. We set up the equipment in about an hour and did a sound check. We were ready to go. Tommy, the owner, seemed like a nice guy, and was not much older than us. He was really enthusiastic about the idea of a show instead of just a dance band.

We were all starving by the time we set up, so we ordered a pizza from the kitchen. Happily, it was good. It's handy to play places that have a kitchen, especially if the food is good. Nice work if you can get it. Small town eating is often adventurous. Even though we were so often in the hinterlands, where farming is a way of life, it was often hard to get a decent meal. To some extent, we figured this was because most people in small towns ate supper at home. Certainly, home cooking was something we missed on the road. But there were other factors.

For example, restaurants often used "coffee whitener" instead of cream, and wheat toast was looked on as a socialist conspiracy. In the country! One would think that if anywhere, cream would be served with coffee in the country, and wheat toast would be common. The opposite turned out to be true and I, for one, found that I could get better meals in the city. It wasn't that people in the country had forgotten what good food is so much as they seemed to have bought in to the false convenience presented by such things as powdered whitener for coffee and jelly in little plastic packages. Even so, we found that the best restaurants in the small towns we passed through were the breakfast places. Besides these, it was rare in the towns we played to find a restaurant that served anything on a plate for dinner, except for bars. And if there was no bar, burger-and-fry stands were the norm. If we were lucky.

We opened to a good crowd that night, and for Monday in any small town that was good news. Tommy's wasn't very big, and that made it look more packed. People in the audience were mostly young, like us. In most places, there was a good cross-section of ages. But not here. It seemed as if the older people had stayed home, leaving the young ones to party. Everyone liked Bobby, and they liked the dance sets as well. The Love Machine was hot.

After the show that night, we were ready to party ourselves, but all the townies went home. They had to get up to go to work the next day. We went to the club's kitchen to see if there was anything to eat. The cooks and waitresses were closing up and were fixing themselves sandwiches. They offered to fix us some, too. Yes, ma'am! We dug in. Good folks. Barry got to talking with Tommy, and talked him out of a quart of Jack Daniels Green Label. Who could complain? Happy and well fed, we went back to the Skyview to have a drink.

Next morning, we were up early – I say "early" – and drove to town in Bob's van for breakfast by ten. It was just the four of us. Bobby and Hollywood wouldn't even think of getting out of bed until two or three, although Hollywood sometimes got up before noon.

Quite a place, the restaurant. The only place. Just an old-fashioned beanery with a high, stamped-metal ceiling. The menu was standard fare – no socialist toast. It was filled with plaid shirts and baseball caps of all ages. We city boys couldn't help but stick out, but it was OK. Everyone was friendly and talkative. People figured we were with the band for that Elvis guy that had blown into town, and made the usual small talk: Where we were from? What instrument did we play? How did we get into this? And we learned about them, too. It was nice to sit in the morning and relax over coffee. It reminded me of Jo Ann's or Kamel's, some of the greasy spoons we surveyors frequented for breakfast.

Charles and Bob planned to go to the pool hall afterwards, and talked Barry into going, too. I wasn't really wild about it, but I had no way back to the motel except walking. Or a taxi. Heh-heh.

The pool hall was the single worst, most disgusting place I have ever been.

Its outside was an old storefront, the windows dingy. Right inside was an old glass merchandise case. It was mostly empty, save for a few ten-cent combs, nail clipper key chains, and stuff. No more gum and cigars. There was about forty years' worth of dust on it, and everywhere else. The light coming in the front picture windows seemed filtered through amber. The few hanging bare bulbs were dim. More dim, maybe, than the blue daylight seeping in through the dirty windows at the back of the room.

The floors were heavy, dark wood planks, like in an old feed store. The walls were some kind of plaster, long since turned dark yellow by dust, cigarette and cigar smoke, and the ceiling was too dark to tell. Wooden rafters, I think. But then there were the tables.

They were great. The one redeeming factor. Old-style, nine-footers with slate beds. The billiard tables had leather net pockets, not runways and coin slots, and there were some honest-to-goodness snooker tables. These had no pockets. Some of the tables had red felt instead of green. About a dozen tables all told, and they sat heavily on the floor toward the back of the hall.

The man who ran the place was in the same shape as the display case. Old and doddering, kind of heavy set, with white hair and pasty skin. He wandered about the place keeping track of games. There were some local boys – teens – playing, and he seemed to know them all. Often, he talked to himself, and he had a long, wet stain down the right leg of his grey pants. Every now and then he would call out to no one in particular, "Who's for puss? I! I!"

I watched the others play for a while, and even played a game myself. Charles and I played Bob and Barry. We won.

By now, it was a little after noon, and, amazingly, Bobby and Hollywood showed up. While Hollywood went to eat, Bobby challenged Charles to a game.

The hustler in Bobby came through immediately. He did all he could to cut Charles, including taunting him. As Bob would say later, "Hell of a way to treat someone who works hard for you."

"Yeah, I used to hustle pool," Bobby explained between shots. "That's how I got this scar across my forehead," he said, pointing to a nasty gash that ran nearly the width of his brow. "I took some sucker's paycheck away from him and he whacked me with a pool cue. Heh-heh."

The others showed no signs of tiring, but I'd had about enough. The hall was dark and depressing, and the smell was like every other pool hall, only worse: stale tobacco and weak kidneys. I decided to walk back to the motel.

I was glad I did. It was not hot or humid. The sky was clear blue, sunny. The main drag through town took a right at the north end, went a block or two, past a church, some houses, then took a left leading down the long hill to the motel. It only took a few minutes to get out of Glasgow. Walking along the road, it was quiet, the kind of quiet where bird songs and bug noises seem loud and you can hear a car coming from half a mile away. I took off my shirt and reveled in the air and the birds. I was back at the Skyview in about twenty minutes.

In the motel room I made some coffee and read. There was nothing on TV. I needed that little piece of solitude. But it was too nice a day to stay inside, so I took a hike in the soybean fields. I found railroad tracks to walk on and signs of surveyors – some stakes and a benchmark (a fixed point of known elevation). Survey spore! Just no getting away. As much as I wanted to get out of surveying, it had made its mark on me. There is something neat about knowing what all those stakes, markers and flags mean, like hidden clues to the puzzle of the world.

After the gig that night Ruby, the bartender, invited us to a party at her place. Everybody there had either been to see the show or worked at Tommy's. It was the usual drinking, smoking, and talking. There weren't a lot of people, but it was a happy diversion just to socialize. Spending so much time between the bar and the motel often left us feeling cut off from civilization. Ruby was our age, not married, not in any relationship far as we could tell, and knew how we felt. And maybe she and her friends needed to meet some new people. Ruby was one of those salt-of-the-earth people we would meet on our travels.

It was an uneventful week. The shows went fine, with good crowds, and friendly people. Tommy was happy with us. Days were quiet, if not boring. Not a lot to do in Glasgow. There were only two restaurants (not counting Tommy's), one for breakfast and one for dinner (and it closed about seven). And there was the old drugstore for sodas.

Inevitably, Saturday came and we geared up for the last night. We were awakened about eight-thirty or nine to the sounds of cars coming and going, people talking and kids laughing. So much for sleeping late our last morning. Charles and I got out of bed and looked out the window. Seemed that there was going to be a wedding in town that day. Our first clue was that every other room in the motel but ours swarmed with people in tuxedos and gowns. They walked up and down the walk from room to room, talking and laughing in expectation. Later, after the wedding, the caravan cruised the back roads between towns. All afternoon, at various intervals, they would pass us by on the road wherever we were – at the motel, in Glasgow – horns honking, streamers streaming. We couldn't help but notice, but didn't pay much attention, except to wave at them whenever they passed.

Later that afternoon, we took a last tour of the town, hitting all the high points. We'd hardly seen Bobby or Hollywood. Of course, we couldn't miss one last soda at the drugstore. Then we walked to the old historic pier at the river, and ceremoniously skipped stones on the wide Missouri. About six, we went for one last hot meal at the restaurant before it closed for the night. I don't even remember what we ate.

After dinner, we strolled along the sidewalk to the club, about a block south. The sidewalks were right out of a western: boardwalks elevated off the street covered by a wooden awning attached the old brick buildings, which were all in a row.

We cast long shadows in the setting sun. Even the Missouri River, languidly rolling behind the buildings across the street, seemed ready to pack it in for the evening. There was no one else out on the street.

Except for the wedding party. About two blocks behind us, we heard the celebratory noise and turned to see them parading down the middle of the street, laughing and talking. They had just made that sharp bend onto the main drag at the north end of town. The groom was pulling the bride in a little red wagon, followed by the wedding entourage.

Being in no hurry, we ambled along, talking and watching over our shoulders. Soon, the wedding party came up even to us, but paid us no mind. We, however, paused, standing still to watch the parade.

Suddenly, the groom stopped, and so did the wedding party. They were all in a festive mood, laughing, talking, and drinking champagne from the bottle. He leaned down and said something to the bride, then turned to continue. He gave a hefty tug on the wagon tongue.

His new bride tumbled backwards out of the wagon, onto the street.

On her ass.

In her white wedding gown.

She was pissed.

And embarrassed.

And livid.

She stood up, still clutching her bridal bouquet in one hand, hoisted her gown with the other, threw a dagger look at the groom, and stalked back the other way in her white high heels, crying. Everyone else stood watching in the middle of the street, stunned, frozen, mouths agape. Finally, the groom snapped out of it and ran after her, pleading.

"But honey..."

She was having none of it. The bride kept on, rounding the bend without looking back, the forlorn groom following. A long, sorry silence passed before the rest of the entourage looked at each other, bewildered, and straggled after, one of them dragging the wagon.

We watched until they, too, rounded the bend, out of sight. The four of us looked at each other, also. Without a word about the strange tableau, we went on to Tommy's and drank until show time.

As usual, we kicked ass. Bobby was great, Hollywood sold out of pictures, and he found a girlfriend for the night. Afterwards, as we packed up, some of the folks invited us to a party, a fish fry on the sandbar on the river. Hollywood and Bobby accepted. We politely declined. We were ready for home.

Before driving back to the Skyview, we waved good-bye

and some of the people thanked us for the good time. One guy, who had been there at Tommy's nearly all week, whom we recognized and had gotten to like, looked at me and said, "Well, whatever it is you're looking for, I hope you find it."

We slept at the motel before making the drive back to Kansas City. Really, we had wanted to leave right after packing, but we were all too tired. Asleep at the wheel. On the road by seven-thirty a.m., it was a sunny morning for a drive.

Silence reigned as we curved along the back roads, heading for the interstate. Everyone was always numb after a week of working and living together. Hollywood and Bobby, of course, had the truck and trailer.

As we hit I-70, the conversation picked up.

"Well, I wonder how that party was," began Barry. "They were gonna have a fish-fry." He sounded kind of wistful.

"I'm sure we'll get a report from Hollywood," answered Bob, eyes on the road, hands on the wheel, lips on the joint. "I wouldn't have minded going, but –"

"But dammit," Barry picked up, "we were there all week, and nothing. The night we're gonna leave it's 'Hey, let's party!' That always happens."

"Yeah," said Charles, "but those people work during the week."

"But jeez," said Barry, "they could have had it Friday night."

"And by Saturday," Bob threw in, "we're so sick of the town we don't want to stay and party."

"Let's face it," I concluded, "the people were nice, but the place was boring."

"And besides, we've all got someone to go home to," stressed Charles.

"True," said Bob. "Bobby is pretty much on the loose. Home is where the show is. And Hollywood too. But that's the thing about the road: It's kind of a vagabond life. Living out of a suitcase. It's no way to live if you're in a relationship. The guy I used to travel with, Tommy Riggs, was on the road nine months a year. It was rare that he got home to Little Rock to see his family. But he sure liked the road."

"Makes for kind of a double existence," I said. "Here you have this thing that you like, playing music, and it takes you away from everything else. Sort of doesn't make any sense. I guess it wouldn't be as bad if we were going to neat places, like Hawaii."

"Or Japan," said Bob. "Fat chance."

"But we're artists," emphasized Charles. "We've got to play. Would you want to go back to work for the City, Frank? Or the warehouse, Barry? We've got to keep that in mind. We're a good band, I think we can make it."

"We could be on the road forever, though, Charles. Who's gonna find us?" I asked.

"Well," said Bob, "I figure that if we hang together that maybe, just maybe, we could work our way out to Vegas or even California. It's a long shot with Bobby. He may get shot next time we play the Monroe Inn or something, and his management is lousy. Look at Lee. He fucks up more jobs than he gets. And Jerry Plantz. He's only interested in his commission. But still, Bobby's good enough to play Vegas, and we're good enough to back him. I mean, Tommy Riggs played Vegas!"

He sighed. "I'm not counting on any of this, you understand. When you think of it, how far can he go with an act like this which is, essentially, grave robbing? He said he wanted to record, but who'd buy an imitation Elvis album?"

"He'd be good if he did his own show," added Charles. "Get away from Elvis and just do a nightclub act. He's got a good voice, and he knows how to put a show together. But he won't listen to us."

By now we had talked up an appetite. We jumped off the freeway at a Nickerson Farms restaurant. As an extra-added attraction, this one had a beehive built into the narrow end of the building, near the entrance. There was about a four-foot Plexiglas bubble over the hive, inside and out, to keep the bees from swarming off. They could go from the sunny outside to the fluorescent lighting inside for warmth in the winter. Certainly, they were busy worker bees, producing honey for sale in the restaurant's gift shop. I bought a Sunday Kansas City Star so I could begin to get back in touch with the world at large.

It hadn't blown up yet. And breakfast tasted great. We took our time. Monday we were free and Tuesday back on road.

He Don't Look Like Elvis

Where The Hell Is Poplar Bluff?

IT WAS NOT JUST A RHETORICAL question: Where the hell is Poplar Bluff? It was a bumper sticker. Real popular in Poplar Bluff, which, by the way, is down in southeast Missouri.

Poplar was kind of a stopgap gig. There wasn't anything going on in Kansas City, and Bobby didn't want to leave us without work for a week. And, actually, we didn't want Bobby to leave us without work.

The deal was, the Love Machine would go play the gig without Bobby while he stayed in Kansas City to present trophies at the Benjamin Stables rodeo. Hollywood would either help Bobby or have the week off.

Charles, Bob, and Barry met at my house Tuesday morning, and we took off about six-thirty. Poplar Bluff was an eight-hour drive. We were supposed to open that night. Any accident or breakdown of vehicles would have fucked us for sure.

The drive from Kansas City to Springfield, especially down Highway 13, was familiar, at least for Bob and me. We're Missouri boys, and the Ozarks is familiar ground. But none of us had ever been to Poplar. The rolling, mountainous southern Missouri countryside was wonderful. Highway 60, the road east out of Springfield, wound through hills thick with hickory and hackberry trees, and eventually pines were mingled in as we got to Mark Twain National Forest. Really a beautiful drive, but we had no time for sightseeing.

Charles and I were in charge of the pickup and trailer, while Barry rode in the van with Bob. As Charles would soon discover, as Hollywood and I had on the way to Minot, it was a cantankerous contraption to drive. Charles hadn't really driven it any distance until this trip. The gauges still hadn't been fixed. True, it might have been nothing more than blown fuses, but it was Lee's truck, and Bobby and Hollywood did most of the driving in it. Ergo, we weren't around it enough to think of fuses. So we still had to depend on Bob to know when to stop for gas. We were on a tight schedule, and Bob was in no mood to hang back on our account. It was hard enough just keeping up with him on a four-lane interstate. On a two-lane like Highway 60, passing some of the slowpokes we encountered was downright nerve-wracking.

It was about four p.m. when we hit town, going south on U.S. 67. It was one of the main drags on the west side of Poplar Bluff, a town of about 20,000. We were just in time for rush hour. The city had that kind of suburban look to it: no tall buildings, and the roads seemed like one big strip mall. There were so many business signs it looked like a forest.

The Embers Lounge was easy enough to find. It was right on the east side of the highway. We stopped long enough to get directions to the motel. We'd played a lot of boring-looking clubs in our brief travels, and this was another one.

Marlene, the owner-bartender, told us where the motel was. "Go on down the highway, take a left at the last light."

It was a decent-looking place on the edge of town, run by some old man and his wife. We walked into the office and told the woman who we were.

"Oh, yes, I was expecting you. But you'll have to pay for the rooms in advance. $42.73 apiece." It was obvious she just didn't trust traveling musicians. N'er-do-wells and scalawags all. Carpetbaggers.

We all looked at each other, and shrugged. This wasn't in the deal; the club was supposed to pay the motel. Luckily, we all had some money. Each of us paid our share to the old woman, with Charles asking his usual "Which way is north?" I gave the woman exact change, but:

"Do you have another penny?" the woman asked, pushing one of them back to me. "My bank won't take these."

I blinked at her in disbelief. Here I'd just given her two twenties, two ones, a quarter, five dimes and three pennies pulled randomly from my pocket. All genuine United States currency, trusting in God, e pluribus, and all that. The penny was equally valid, just a little road-worn, nicked and scratched. Not even bent. And here this asshole bumpkin wants me to give her another because her "bank won't take these." What, she sees a lot of "these"?

In my most calculated, deadpan insolence, I stared at her and said "No." Of course, I lied. It was real quiet for a minute, as she mulled over a response. I was ready to stand my ground. Indeed, I was readying a tirade on the penny's behalf. Bob, Charles and Barry were staring at us. Just as the woman seemed about to speak, Charles broke in.

"Wait. I have one here," and handed her a shiny new one. I gave the offender to Charles, and all was right with the world. Hard to believe the balance can hang by a penny.

The rooms were not big, but nice enough with requisite dark wood paneling. Two to a room, as usual: Bob and Barry; Charles and I. We dumped our stuff and went back to The Embers to set up. The bar was all but uninhabited, save for Marlene and two customers playing pool.

"Hmm, we might be able to set up all of us on the stage," mused Charles, eyeing the triangular, six-inch-high platform fitted into one corner of the dance floor. "But look at this carpet!" he went on. "It looks like a pig sty!"

Indeed, the carpet on the stage was littered with broken strings, used guitar picks, cigarette butts and matches.

"I'll see if I can get someone to clean it up," said Bob. He went over to the bar to talk to Marlene. He came back.

"She says there's a vacuum."

A few minutes later Marlene unceremoniously plopped the vacuum on the stage, and went back to the bar. We went on setting up the PA and stringing wires, naively thinking that someone was going to come run the vacuum. But after a while, it dawned on us.

"I don't think anyone's coming," said Charles.

"Well, I'm not going to vacuum their damned stage for them," fumed Bob.

We worked a little more.

"Looks like a Mexican standoff," said Barry. Disgusted, we put the machine on the dance floor, and set up the rest of our stuff. Fuck the stage. We did, however, consider working the vacuum into the act.

Fortunately, it was a slow opening night. Without Bobby, half the show was missing. That meant we had to play four sets of material with barely enough to cover two. It was like the five loaves and two fishes. There was a lot of song repetition and stretching. It took a couple of nights, but we got the hang of it, and no one seemed to notice.

Days were slow. There wasn't much to do except wake up and go eat, and there was no place exciting to go do that. One afternoon, we went to shoot Barry's Ruger .22 automatic. This trip, for a change of pace, he'd left his two friends home and opted for lighter firepower. We bought some ammo at a hardware store and, following directions from the hardware store guy, found a creek not far from the motel on the outskirts of town. It was down a gravel road that crossed one of those old girder and plank bridges. Standing on the bridge, we threw cans and bottles into the water and tried to sink them. We were all pretty fair shots, actually. Fully armed, we could have shot our way out of any bar we played in.

It might as well have been called The Dying Embers. In the course of shooting the shit with Marlene, who really was a decent sort, Bob found out that after our week there the place would close. Just not enough business.

We could see why. For one thing, there was no kitchen. No going to The Embers for dinner and dancing. And the place looked boring, although no more boring than any other place we worked.

Maybe it was the town itself. Maybe there was no club scene in Poplar Bluff. I mean, in our position we couldn't investigate the nightlife. For all I know, we were the nightlife of Poplar Bluff. Actually, there were some other clubs in town. But the music, according to our conversations with Embers customers and our daily forays, was either very sterile Holiday Inn disco, or country. We were somewhere in between.

By the latter part of the week, we were drawing better crowds. Generally, they liked to get up and dance, didn't complain about our song stretching, and liked the band's selections. However, they weren't a late-night bunch, and it was rare that any but a few people stayed through the end of the last set at one a.m., if they even made it that far.

There were a few customers lingering Thursday night as we prepared to go back to the motel for the night. None of us thought much of it. A few guys, a few women.

We were just about to get in Bob's van when this woman walked up to us. I recognized her as one of the lingerers. She wore black corduroy pants, and a white blouse with a black velour string tie. About five-four, light brown hair.

"Could I get a ride home?" she asked. She seemed a little unsure.

"A ride?" asked Bob, his brow wrinkled.

"Yeah. I came with my brother and his wife, and they left me."

"Why'd they leave you?" asked Bob, wary.

"He has to get up early. Do you think I could get a ride?"

We all looked at each other. Was this some sort of come-on? She didn't seem drunk. Weird visions came to mind, not all of them exciting. She was staring at us.

"It's his van," I said, thumbing toward Bob. "He'll have to decide."

Bob looked at me. "What do you think, Frankie Stone?"

I shrugged. It might be wild. None of us had said ten words to anybody other than our fellow band members and Marlene all week.

"Well," sighed Bob, "what the hell. OK, you can have a ride. Where do you live?"

"Well," she said in her soft southern Missouri accent, pointing in the general direction of the motel, "just go down the highway here until you get to Moreland, and take a left. I'll tell you from there."

"Hop in," said Bob. He looked skeptical. She got in the shotgun seat, the rest of us cluttering in back. Charles, I could tell, was on the verge of being scandalized.

As we neared Moreland, Bob asked which way to go.

"Take a right."

"I thought you said take a left."

"Well . . . I forget."

Sitting in the back of the van with Charles, Barry and I looked at each other and rolled our eyes. Charles shook his head.

At Moreland there was a traffic light, and Bob stopped for a red. "All right now, which way is it?" He was beginning to smell a fiasco.

"Well, could we go to your motel instead?"

"What?!?"

"Maybe I could phone my brother. He was going to Sambo's."

"Doesn't he have to work in the morning?"

"He wasn't going to stay late."

"OK, OK, we'll go to the motel," said Bob finally, humoring her. Barry and I raised our eyebrows. Yes, seems we had a live one. Her name was Cathy.

"I'm going to sleep, you guys," said Charles as we got out of the van. He went into his (and my) room. The rest of us went into Bob and Barry's room.

"There's the phone," said Bob, pointing. There was even a phone book.

"I'll call in a little bit," Cathy said. She sat on Bob's bed, and I sat next to her. Barry sat on his bed; Bob took a chair.

"Well," asked Bob, being conversational, "what do you do here in Poplar Bluff?"

"I'm a secretary," Cathy answered quietly.

"Are you married?" I asked, noticing the wedding ring on her finger.

"No," she smiled, holding it up. "I just wear it so they'll let me in bars."

"How old are you?" I asked.

"Nineteen."

"Going on seventeen?" teased Bob. Cathy giggled.

Barry turned on the TV. We all seemed a little nervous. We weren't trying to quiz her, but we had to start somewhere. Besides, we would have been glad to answer her questions, but she didn't ask any. Cathy wasn't much for conversation.

Maybe she wanted us to gang-bang her, or maybe she wanted to talk. Whatever it was, she didn't know how to go about getting us to do it. She seemed unsure of what she wanted. And none of us was just going to jump her without more of an invitation. Especially in a strange town to boot. I pushed it.

Slowly, I undid her tie, and unbuttoned her blouse while kissing the back of her neck.

She didn't kiss back. She didn't move a muscle.

Hmm. I was a might bewildered.

I undid her sleeves and took off her blouse, then unsnapped her bra (two-finger technique), but didn't take it off. Never once did Cathy make any complaint, at which point I would have stopped. But she didn't help, either. I rubbed her back. Barry watched the TV.

By this time, Bob had stripped down to his shorts.

"Listen," he said, "I'm going to bed. If you two want to hump, you ain't doing it in my bed."

I thought of taking Cathy over to my room. But the scenario didn't jibe. It was all wrong. Maybe if Cathy had been a little more responsive. But as it was, it didn't seem kosher.

We sat there stupidly.

"Well, hell," said Bob. He walked over to Cathy, standing in front of her. Reaching down, he undid her jeans and pulled them off, and then took off her bra, exposing her good-sized breasts to God and everybody. Their nipples were huge, and Bob stared agog.

"Ole jelly-jar lids!" he exclaimed, clearly amazed.

"What?" I quizzed.

"She's got nipples like ole jelly-jar lids!" he repeated.

"Jelly-jar lids?" I said. We all laughed at that one. Even Cathy, sitting now in nothing but her white satin panties, had to laugh.

Still, she made no counteraction.

Bob was befuddled.

He got into bed and Cathy followed. He tried kissing her, but it wasn't happening. She didn't kiss back.

They both lay side by side for a few minutes. Barry and I watched to see what would happen.

Suddenly, Bob cackled a laugh. "Jesus, I can't do this!" He laughed some more, jumping out of bed. "Look, Cathy, this just isn't happening. We've all got sweeties at home, and we don't know you. More than that, you're not telling us what you want, and I don't think you've been honest with us." He was putting on his clothes. "Get up and get dressed, then call your brother. We'll take you to him."

Cathy looked confused. "He may be gone by now," she whined.

"Then we'll take you home. You can't stay here, OK?"

Slowly she got up and dressed. She called Sambo's.

"He doesn't seem to be there."

"Well, come on, we'll take you where you need to go," said Bob. He was more exasperated than unkind.

We all piled into the van.

"OK now, where's home?" demanded Bob.

"Go back down the highway past Sambo's."

"I thought you lived close to here?" Bob was wearing thin.

"Well..."

"OK, where do you want to go?" Bob snapped.

"Take me by Sambo's. I'll see if my brother is there."

We headed for Sambo's.

Right across the street from it, on the same side of the highway, was a parking lot. Cathy pointed to a Chevy Blazer parked near the corner of the lot.

"There's my car," she said. "Let me out here. OK?"

"Sure, no problem," said Bob. He wheeled into the lot. Still, Cathy seemed reluctant to go.

Bob hugged her.

"You know," he said soothingly, trying to let her down easy, "normally, any one of us would have been back there fucking your lights out. But it doesn't seem right. Do you understand?"

She nodded, opened the door and got out.

"Sorry Cathy," Bob said.

"Take care," I called after.

Cathy shrugged. "Bye now." She closed the door and walked to her Blazer. We sat as she drove off, back in the general direction she had first told us – Moreland and the motel.

Bob waited quietly a few minutes, to give Cathy a chance to put some distance between us. I got in the shotgun seat.

"Jeez, what a deal!" breathed Bob. We all sighed.

"Ha!" I said. "Nineteen! Not married!"

"Yeah," agreed Bob. "That's all we need – some jealous husband to shoot us on stage. Atchison all over!"

"Oh well," I philosophized, "so much for sex, drugs, and rock 'n' roll."

Bob began singing the old spiritual, "Nobody knows the weirdness I've seen . . ."

". . . on the trail of the Brown Buffalo," I finished.

The next morning, Friday, we went back to Sambo's for breakfast. It was the only place we knew of. We had gotten up early so we could go to Mark Twain National Forest, just north of town.

"God, what a weird night," said Barry. Bob and I just grunted.

"So," taunted Charles, "did you guys take that girl to Bob's room and screw her?"

Barry looked down at his coffee.

"Charles," I said, "someday we'll tell you the whole story. Heh-heh."

"You guys . . ."

Just then, the waitress came to take our orders.

We shared the newspapers while waiting for our food. Gosh, we had the St. Louis Post Dispatch and The Kansas City Star. Uptown. Charles was in good spirits as usual. He laughed all the way through the funnies.

"Yeah," broke in Barry, "but did you check out Ann Landers?"

About halfway through the meal, I brought up a touchy subject, about which the others had no way of knowing about.

"Gee, guys, I don't know how to say this but . . ."

"You're pregnant," interrupted Barry.

"No, but close. It's my birthday."

"Hey man," grinned Charles, patting me on the back. "Happy birthday!"

"Does this mean you want us to buy your breakfast?" joked Bob.

Barry laughed. "No, he's going to buy ours."

Heh-heh.

"How old are you?" asked Bob.

"Twenty-seven."

"An old man!" said Bob.

"Do you feel older?" asked Barry.

"No, just better. But it makes me think . . ."

We fell into our usual discussion. Where is this taking us? Why bands?

"What's it all mean, Mr. Natural?" queried Barry.

I gave the proper answer. "Don't mean shee-it."

Then it hit me. In a flash, I could see the future of being on the road in somebody else's band: Traveling for years, no home, no social life, no getting anywhere but old.

"Wait!" I exclaimed. "I could go back to school!"

"Man," grinned Charles, "that would be great. Have you gone before?"

"Yeah, I had two years. I could go back as a junior. Be out in no time!"

"What would you major in?" asked Bob.

"Well, I've got an associate degree, kind of toward an English major. But I'm sure there's something else I could take. I don't want to teach. Now, I bet I could figure it out."

"Man, that is exciting," agreed Charles. He was genuinely pleased for me.

I made up my mind. "Well, I'll apply as soon as I get home from here." The University of Missouri–Kansas City was a few minutes' drive from my house.

After breakfast, we went back to the hotel and regrouped, getting ready to go to the forest. It was a very clear day, and not too hot.

In about forty minutes, we were in the parking lot for one of the forest hiking trails. We were in good shape, having smoked dope all the way, much to Charles' chagrin.

Mark Twain National Forest covers much of southeast Missouri, and has some of the highest points in the state. And we were near one of them – Eagle Peak.

We had the choice of following the river, or climbing. We checked out the river first.

"Hey, look at this!" cried Bob, skipping stones on the water. Naturally, we all picked up rocks and a contest ensued. It was a tie.

People were floating down the river in canoes and on inner tubes. We waved. They waved back.

"Come on," said Bob. "Let's hike up the mountain."

The trail wound its way up, the sunlight filtering its way through the tall oak and other decidedly deciduous trees. At the bottom portion of the trail, near the river, the mosquitoes were awful.

"Damn!" yelled Barry. "These suckers are bigger than in Florida!"

"Ain't nothing," I said. "Why, when we got out of the van, I seen one of 'em standing flat-footed fuckin' a turkey!"

"Sounds like the Colonel," said Bob catching on. He'd heard some of my survey tales.

"Well, they're eating me alive!" moaned Charles.

"You gotta eat more garlic and Looziana hot sauce," I said. "They don't bother me."

"I hear smoke keeps 'em away," noted Barry, as he lit a joint.

The trail was narrow and dictated single file. The man in front passed the joint back, and whoever was at the end of the line ran up front to take the lead and pass it back. The 500-meter joint relay. Charles' not smoking threw the rhythm off a little, but he was kind enough to pass it along sometimes. After all, he had smoked before.

In any case, the trail soon took a noticeable turn upward, and we were above the mosquito line.

It was a good hike. As we went higher, the trail was more visibly on the slope edge. Every now and then, we passed a clearing where we could look down on the river and see the people floating by. When there were no floaters, we threw rocks to see if we could hit the water.

Yes, we could.

An hour and a half of climbing, and still we were not quite to the top. Maybe three-quarters. We took a rest on a rock ledge.

A tree had grown up on the ledge below, about twenty feet, and the way the bark had grown around the ledge where we were resting made it seem as if the tree was taking a bite out of the rock. Bob took a picture.

"What a view," he sighed, taking a deep breath.

"This is great," said Barry. "There's no place this high in Florida."

I said nothing, but turned my good eye – the surveyor's eye – to scan the countryside. We stood quiet a few minutes, listening to the wind rustling the leaves on the trees. It came in waves. A hawk hovered over the river.

Bob laughed. "Boy, I can see Bobby standing out in the middle of the rodeo arena. In his white suit."

"With a trophy in one hand," joined Barry. We all laughed.

More silence.

"It sure is nice . . ." said Bob, distantly.

"What?" asked Charles.

"To be out in the daytime, in the sun. It's nice – 'cause it's so different, having to work at night. It's nice that we get to have fun outside."

"Yeah," I picked up. "I liked working outside. That was the best part of surveying. No office roof over my head. Of course, we suffered in the bad weather, but the good weather made it all worthwhile. That's how I kept at it so long." I took a breath. "But what a way of life now. We get to play outside. Not work. And it's relaxing, not having Bobby along. The whole of it, though . . ." I trailed off.

"But this is what we do," counseled Charles. "And people like us. We're good."

"But good has nothing to do with it," I came back. "There are plenty of players who are good. Where are they?"

"Where are they?" asked Bob, rhetorically. "They're all working day jobs. I mean, look at the New York scene. About ten guys have all the recording gigs sewed up, and they do a lot of work and make a lot of money. Everybody else plays in clubs for scale, if they're lucky. That leaves us in Poplar Bluff."

"And Bobby at the rodeo," added Barry.

Within half an hour, we were at the top. It wasn't a peak as such, and there weren't any fewer trees, but the view was wonderful. Gazing out, standing still, we soaked up the surroundings.

We rested a spell, checked out the scenery, smoked another joint.

By now it was late afternoon, around three-thirty, and suddenly we were hungry. We had no water, either. Drymouth prevailed. It was sad to leave such great scenery, but we picked ourselves up and continued following the trail on down. There wasn't much stopping for sights – there were steaks before our eyes. At the bottom of the trail, near the end, the land got a little swampy. We passed through the only naturally growing stand of bamboo in the state, according to the sign. Hey, now! There was also a quiet pond with swans swimming, and in the late sun it was wonderful.

But, we were hungry and the swans were off limits.

By the time we got back to the van, we were ravenous.

"Let's go eat," hinted Barry.

"Where should we go?" quizzed Bob.

"How about that Greek place?" I suggested.

We had passed it several times during the week, and the thought of a gyro was quite appealing.

"Naw," vetoed Bob, "I'm suspicious of Greek places. What are they gonna do, stick a steak up your ass?"

"Only if you bend over," I teased. "OK, how about Mexican? There was that place on the highway not far into town."

"You and your tacos," said Charles. "I want pizza."

"With pepperoni and sausage?" I asked.

"No, man, you know I don't eat pork. 'Lips that touch swine . . .'"

" . . . will never touch mine," finished Bob.

"Your what?" taunted Barry. "Pizza sounds good to me. Or how about steak?"

"I haven't seen a steak place here," said Bob. "Not even a Sizzler."

"Grizzler?" I offered.

"God," laughed Bob, "you've got a name for every place."

"All those years of survey," I said.

"Anyway," Bob continued, "I don't mind pizza either."

Barry and Charles agreed.

"Well, Frank, I'm drivin'. You lose," stated Bob.

"Oh man, I don't want pizza on my birthday!"

We hashed it over again. Greek was out. Burgers were out. Barbecue was out. The only barbecue we had seen in town was Coleman's. But it had no atmosphere. The place was like a fast-food barbecue joint.

Besides, it wasn't as good as Kansas City barbecue. On that we all agreed.

My first encounter with Coleman's was when Anne and

I were on our way to Biloxi, Mississippi, to visit her aunt and uncle, a couple of years earlier. We'd stopped in Jonesboro, Arkansas, and Coleman's looked good. We had barbecue beef sandwiches.

Actually, they were quite tasty, except that they put coleslaw on the damned sandwich. Coleslaw! They'd be laughed out of Kansas City! My first thought was that they were trying to cut down on the beef.

Next time we went through Jonesboro, I was ready. No slaw. So, when we spied a Coleman's in Poplar Bluff, I warned everybody when we went to eat there.

"I like it that way," said Bob.

"You mean they're not trying to skimp on the meat?"

"No, man, that's how they do it in the South. It's good." And he'd been to a Coleman's.

"Fuck the South. What do they know?" I was indignant. "They lost the Civil War, didn't they? You just don't put coleslaw on barbecue sandwiches! Fuck 'em, I say!"

Like I said, Coleman's was out.

"Tell you what," said Bob, being cooperative. "We'll leave you at the Mexican place, and we'll go get pizza. OK?"

"OK."

The prospect of birthday dinner by myself didn't really appeal to me, but I wanted tacos alone more than pizza with company. That's how I came to be eating tacos alone in a Mexican restaurant in Poplar Bluff, Missouri, on Friday, my twenty-seventh birthday.

The tacos weren't bad, but not anything to write home about. And I was about the only person in the place. I guess because it was that time between the lunch and dinner rushes. The windows were a mosaic of thick, multicolored glass, like red, blue, yellow, and green Coke bottle bottoms. The late afternoon sun streaming in made for great light. The nice-looking waitress was not overly friendly or attentive. Leisurely, I stuffed myself.

Happy birthday.

After eating, I went outside to wait for the others. The pizza place was about a half a block away. Before long, they showed up, full and happy, and we went back to the motel to get ready for work.

That night, the crowd was pretty thin. And no sign of Cathy, either, or any groupies at all. Our biggest crowds had been Wednesday and Thursday. Not standing-room-only, but enough to keep the dance floor busy. It was a challenge arranging sets but we had figured out how to stretch two sets worth of songs into four. On Tuesday, our first night, we played the first set and the second set, then used the first for the third set and the second for the fourth set. The next night, we started with the second set first.

Then we made completely new sets. At one point, we considered drawing songs out of a hat. In short, we milked each song for all it was worth, which was not much for most of them. We stretched any solo we could to the breaking point.

No matter what we did, it was like eating bad leftovers. Unfortunately, none of us knew the words to the Elvis songs that Bobby sang or we would have done those.

Amazingly, neither Marlene nor the audience complained. In any case, on Friday there was hardly enough audience to complain. Maybe everyone in town knew that The Embers was dying. Maybe it was never popular.

Marlene insisted on playing the jukebox to an empty house during our breaks, following the rule of never allowing a moment of silence. Marlene probably needed the noise herself. The jukebox was far and away louder than we were. At least Marlene didn't demand that we feed the jukebox. Some owners did, though we rarely caved in. It was our job to provide live music. If they wanted the jukebox played, they had to cough up the quarters. If the patrons don't even care enough to play the jukebox, a joint is really dead.

We didn't look forward to our breaks. They were more boring than playing to tables and chairs. When we weren't out back of the club smoking hash, which I had obtained for this outing, Charles and Bob would kill time playing pool. Barry sometimes did too. I brought something to read. Too bad there wasn't a kitchen for a snack. Maybe that was another reason the bar wasn't making it.

Still, Friday night wasn't a total loss. When we came off stage for our second break, two familiar blondes waved us over to their table. Patsy and Denise were members of the Bobby Love Fan Club. Although we didn't know them well, we recognized those two, true zealots who always showed up at the Monroe Inn and Genova's in Kansas City, and even the Melrose in Atchison. Now they had driven clear to Poplar Bluff! When we explained that Bobby was up in Kansas City handing out trophies at the Benjamin Rodeo, they were disappointed but had a good time anyway. They bought us some drinks, and we sat and talked during our breaks. This was the first time we had really sat and visited with them. It was nice to see people we knew, even in passing.

Before our last set, Patsy took our pictures on stage. She got some individual shots, some random pairs and groups, and the requisite wacky full-band pose. (For some reason, whenever a band – any band – poses for a group shot, the members turn into the Beatles.) She said that she would have them for us in a couple of weeks.

Bright and early Saturday, around seven-thirty or eight, Charles and I were awakened by what sounded like the screeching sound of metal against metal outside our door. What the hell? Charles opened the door, and there was the old man who owned the place. He said he just had to drill into our door to put some new numbers on it, or something. Couldn't wait until we woke up. Jeez! The fucker.

For the rest of the day, we pretty much took it easy, packed our bags, rounded up our stuff. Our plan was to leave right after the show that night. We were tired of Poplar Bluff and the ubiquitous "Where The Hell Is Poplar Bluff?" bumper stickers (one of which was on Bob's van).

Shortly after noon, we went to a gas station to fill up the van and pickup truck and check the tires on the trailer. We bought some oil and transmission fluid to put in the truck later. Then we went to a burger joint for lunch.

On the way out, Bob was in the lead, with Barry in the van with him. He pulled out of the drive to get onto the main road, but traffic was too heavy. He decided to back up a bit. Charles and I were in the truck close behind him, but at a right angle to the van.

Charles was driving. "Damn, Frank, Bob's gonna back into us if he doesn't look out." He couldn't back out of the way quick enough, what with the trailer hooked to the truck and the odd angle, so we yelled out the windows.

Of course, the horn didn't work either.

"Hey Bob," yelled Charles. I whistled and yelled. He kept on backing.

There was barely ten feet between us, and he backed right into the passenger door of the truck, breaking the outside mirror. As soon as he hit, he stopped and got out.

"Oh, shit," he said. The mirror was gone, and there was a nice big dent in the door.

"We tried to tell you, Bob," said Charles, "but the horn doesn't work."

"Yeah, and I couldn't hear you yelling," he said, mournfully. "We had the windows up and the AC blowing." Lucky them. There was no AC in that truck. And if there had been, it, too, wouldn't have worked.

Oh well. We decided to fix the mirror because it was necessary for driving. The dent, well, maybe Lee would never notice. It fit in with the overall decor.

We went back to the motel and played catch in the lot behind the motel. We'd all brought our baseball gloves, just in case. Later that afternoon, before we went to dinner, Charles and I checked out the truck for the trip home. We replaced the mirror, having bought one at the local auto parts store on the way back from lunch. Then we tried to kick out the dent in the door, without success.

I put in two quarts of oil – it used that much just for the ride down – and half a quart of transmission fluid. Then I crawled under the truck to see if anything was leaking or loose, which was a distinct possibility. It was the first time we had checked this out, since Bobby and Hollywood mostly drove the truck.

"God damn! Charles! Get under here and look at this!" I yelled.

"What is it?"

"There's no bell housing cover." This bowl-shaped cover protected the transmission's flywheel and other internal parts from road dirt, rocks and debris.

He crawled under to look. "Great," said Charles, as we stared at the flywheel hanging out in space, for all the world to see. "No speedometer, no gauges, no bell housing cover. Bobby's sent us out in a death trap."

Bob and Barry also had a look. "About as much as I expected from Bobby and Lee," Bob dryly observed.

We cleaned up and went to dinner. In the van. For tonight's menu, we had unanimously picked Long John Silver's. Or, as Bob, who had some names of his own, called it, "Long John Silverfish."

"Good God," laughed Bob, as I sloshed malt vinegar on

the fish and chips. "Like a little fish with your vinegar?"

"Soak them suckers," I retorted. I think of fish and chips as a vinegar delivery system, in the same way that any barbecued meat is a sauce delivery system.

Oddly, it was one of our better meals in Poplar Bluff. Afterward, we went next door to the carnival in the huge Ben Franklin Stores parking lot.

There were three midways plus rides. We rode the Ferris wheel, tried a few games. The shooting gallery was a hit with us. There was one midway with nothing but games of chance – ring toss, knock over a stack of milk bottles with a softball, and various others, all designed to take one's money. These games were all run by loud, brassy teenaged girls, practiced in the art of seduction.

"Hey, baby, try your luck . . ."

"Say there, good-lookin', win me a teddy bear!"

"[Wolf-whistle]! Honey, come over here!"

And on and on. In no time at all, we were giving them shit back, laughing all the way, and they were laughing with us.

"Ya gotta lotta nerve, baby!" "Hey, girl, what you got on . . . yo' mind? Heh-heh." And other popular Bobby Love sayings.

Bob and I looked at each other. "Can you believe this shit, man?" he laughed.

"Hey," I said, "They want us to fuck 'em."

"Sheeiiit!" said Bob. "I wouldn't fuck 'em with Charles' dick."

Finally, we were on stage for Saturday night. It was our last night at The Embers. And it was The Embers' last night, period. During the second and third sets, we thought there might be a crowd developing.

But no. By the end of the third set, there were about five couples, and a few strays. All night, our breaks had been getting longer. The fourth set lasted less than thirty minutes. Like that tree falling alone in the forest, no one was there to hear us. There would be no eleventh-hour rallies, no miracle field goals, no stoking of The Embers.

One o'clock came, and that was all she wrote for The Embers and us. After using the bathroom to change into our street clothes, we began tearing down the equipment while Bob went to get the money.

Presently, Bob came back to the bandstand shaking his head, a weird smile on his face.

"What's up?" asked Barry.

"We only got eight hundred dollars for the week."

"So?" asked Charles.

"We were supposed to get fourteen hundred."

"Why didn't we?" I asked.

"Well," explained Bob, "when I went to get the money, I was talking to Marlene. She said she was sorry that there wasn't more of a crowd all week, but things had been slow lately, and that was why she was closing the joint down. I said, 'It's too bad that Bobby Love couldn't come down with us, we'd probably have done better.' She gave me this funny look, and said, 'You mean, none of you is Bobby Love?' Right there, I knew I'd fucked up. So she only paid us eight hundred, and I told her about Bobby and the show. She was a little pissed, but not at us."

"She thought one of us was Bobby Love?" asked Barry, incredulous.

"Yeah," Bob went on. "See, the contract said 'Bobby Love Show with the Love Machine,' and Lee had signed the contract. Evidently, he didn't mention that Bobby did an Elvis act, and also would be in Kansas City handing out trophies at a rodeo. So, she thought one of us was Bobby Love."

"Gee, if we would have known, we could have drawn straws to see who would play Bobby!" laughed Barry.

"Well, you could've counted me out," laughed Charles.

"So," I asked, "what does this mean for us?"

"The band's gonna get paid," said Bob. "I got the money right here. If Bobby would've told me what was going on, I could have kept my mouth shut. Hell, I could've been Bobby Love! But no! He didn't tell us shit. How were we supposed to know he didn't tell the owner he wasn't coming down? And, he expected to get part of the fourteen hundred. He was gonna get paid for not working. That's bad enough, but I'm sure we could have lived with it. But now, fuck him. At least we'll get paid."

"And we'll have to pay for the motel ourselves?" asked Charles.

"I'm afraid so."

"That asshole," said Barry.

"Like I said," reiterated Bob, "he's not going to get any of this money. We worked all week, and Bobby didn't do shit but go to a rodeo. If he'd told me what was going on, I could have handled it. He didn't, so fuck Bobby Love."

"And the horse he rode in on," I added.

That's show biz.

Soon, everything was packed but the guitars. We were just ready to head out the door, and say good-bye to The Embers when the phone rang at the bar.

"Bob, it's for you," said Marlene. "It's Bobby."

"That son of a bitch," said Bob. "Calling to check up on us." We were standing at the back door, across the room from the bar. "Tell him we're gone." We turned and walked out. Oh sure, we knew we'd hear about it later, but what the hell?

There was no choice but to go back to Kansas City that night. We'd already checked out of the motel. We stopped by Sambo's on the way out of town for breakfast. It was about two forty-five a.m., and it was over eight hours to Kansas City.

"I should have known that fucker'd call," said Bob, slurping his coffee. "Well, he's not getting any money. This ought to make up for trying to collect union dues in Minot." Bob gave each of us our week's loot then and there, partly to ensure that none would go to Bobby, but, more importantly, to ensure that we ourselves would get paid without waiting for Bobby to do it.

Our conversation turned to lighter things, and the food showed up. Breakfast was great. We were on the road by four-fifteen.

Charles dropped me off at home about one-thirty that afternoon. It had been a long, tortuous ride. We were dead tired. He was going to take the truck home with all our stuff because the next day, Monday, we started two weeks at the Monroe Inn. Again.

Monroe Inn Redux

IN SOME WAYS I WAS GLAD, and in some ways not. For starters, a return engagement at the Monroe Inn was not what I would consider a victory lap. And neither did the other members of the Love Machine. It was the kind of place that we wanted to get as far away from as possible. On the upside, we would be in town and not stuck in some motel.

That was also the problem. I was getting used to being away from home and wife. Anne was getting used to my not being around and having the car all to herself. She also had to handle most of the paperwork for bills, but I did as much as I could when I was home.

We never fought or anything, but there was a distance growing. As friends, we made a great pair. Otherwise, it wasn't happening, and the road made it more obvious. Somehow, we had the stupid idea that being on the road might help our marriage. That's not why I went on the road, but we both thought it might help.

You blockhead, Charlie Brown.

I said good-bye to Charles and walked up to my porch.

The front door was open and I could see through the house to the back porch, where Anne was potting some plants.

"Hello!" I called, walking in. Anne came in and gave me a hug.

"Happy birthday!" she sang. "And look," she added, pointing, "here's a cake for you."

"Oh good! What kind? Can I have a piece?"

"Yellow with chocolate icing. And no, you can't have a

piece. Not yet. We're supposed to go to Mom's tonight. They're going to have a party for you."

Anne's family lived in Raytown, a suburb in southeast Kansas City. Her mom, brother, and sister. Her dad had died three years earlier, while Anne and I were in Hawaii.

I was tired from the road, but what the hell. I could sleep the next morning. Anne's folks were good company.

"Well," Anne asked, "where are you guys going next?"

"Two weeks at the Monroe Inn."

"Oh. Well, that won't be too bad. It'll be nice to have you here for a while."

She went out back and finished the plants, while I had some coffee.

For the rest of the afternoon, we loafed around the house until it was time to go.

We had a good time with Anne's folks. I appreciated the party, and for a while I could forget music, the road, and the whole damn thing.

Being at home for a gig was harder and more complicated than being on the road, except the accommodations were better.

Since Anne worked every day and I worked every night, we still saw little of each other. By the time I got up in the morning, she was gone. By the time she got home around five-thirty or six, we had time for dinner and then I was off to the show. When I got home around two a.m., she was sleeping.

If I wanted the car, I had to get up and get Anne to work by eight. On days I had the car, I could run errands, go to the park, go to lunch with Anne, pick her up from work. If she had the car, I tended to take long walks just to get out and exercise. I tried to alternate, sort of, so as to get enough sleep.

Moreover, I never expected her to come to the Monroe Inn just to keep me company. It was too hard to be out that late, night after night, and get up for work.

Besides, how much pseudo-Elvis – or Monroe Inn – could one take?

The band didn't hang out together in town because we saw each other all the time on the road, and every night. And we lived far apart. Barry lived in Excelsior Springs, about thirty miles north. Bob lived up north of the river too, but not quite that far. Charles lived on the east side, and I was over in Westport. If we didn't have band business, like rehearsals or whatever, it was easier to stay home.

I looked forward to most nights, just to be out working and in a crowd.

The Monroe Inn was just as we had left it. Tommy, the owner, still used his Jekyll-and-Hyde closing-time technique. He was the nicest guy in the world all night. Come closing time, about one-fifteen a.m., he turned into a snarling maniac.

"Get out! Come on, you assholes, get out – we gotta close!" He would practically pull the chairs out from under people. The method worked, although steady customers tended to laugh while they were leaving. Not what I'd call good business sense, but maybe Tommy had been burned by Kansas City Liquor Control once too often.

The Mexican restaurant was still next door, and the owners were glad to see us. Not only did they like our music, they liked us. And, they liked our business, since we were big fans of their food. They would have our orders waiting at a table in time for break.

The regulars at the Inn were glad to have us back, and for the first week we had good crowds.

By now, we were starting to see more members of the Bobby Love Fan Club besides Connie, Patsy and Denise. Women started showing up in black T-shirts, with the silver Bobby Love logo on the chest. Connie was the president.

"Fat Connie," as Bobby referred to her. True, Connie was

overweight, but she was an intelligent, decent woman, even if she did get vicarious thrills from an Elvis clone. Who were we to knock it? Hell, we worked for him. Nonetheless, while we liked Connie personally, we quickly tired of her hugging and kissing us all the time. Admittedly, if she had been stacked we probably wouldn't have tired so quickly. But we were always nice to Connie and took time to shoot the breeze with her.

We never knew how many people were in the fan club, but after it started more and more members always showed up wherever we played.

Even though the Monroe Inn was where it all began, the crowds began to thin out by the second week. It seemed like a pattern. None of the local clubs we played seemed to serve a big enough radius to sustain the excitement. In any case, Barry, Charles, Bob, and I weren't fooled. We saw this gig for what it was: another stopgap.

Just like sending us to Poplar Bluff was a way for Bobby to keep the band working. And I, for one, didn't mind. Just the threat of a week without work was enough to make us think about new jobs. At the Monroe Inn, we covered no new ground, but it paid the rent.

Bobby didn't forget the Poplar Bluff incident, either.

Our first night at the Monroe Inn, he grilled us.

"Why didn't you guys answer the phone?" he asked Bob.

"We were gone."

He had cornered Bob in the dressing room, that is, the Monroe Inn's broom closet. Bob told me later.

Bobby also quizzed me that night.

"What happened down there in Poplar Bluff?"

"What do you mean?"

"I called and you guys wouldn't talk to me."

"I didn't know you called."

"Oh, come on. You guys couldn't have been gone at the time I called."

"Sorry Bobby." If I had learned anything working for the city, it was how to stonewall.

And we found out about Bobby's big rodeo gig, too.

He had to give out trophies in the rain. In the mud and horseshit. In his white suit. Heh-heh.

I made good on my plan for going back to college. The Tuesday after we got home from Poplar Bluff, our first week at the Monroe Inn, I went to apply at UMKC. I got there late in the morning, about eleven. It was a bright, clear day, not too hot. The campus had several white, two-story wood-frame buildings that looked like Army barracks. In fact, they were Army barracks. In 1948 they had been moved from Camp Crowder Army Base in Neosho, Missouri, to what was then the University of Kansas City. I found University Admissions in one of these.

I reached the second floor office by an exterior wooden staircase. As I went in, a young woman with long blond hair standing behind the counter looked up and greeted me with a friendly smile. I told her I wanted to apply for the fall semester, and might be able to start as a junior because I'd earned an associate degree at Penn Valley Community College in 1972. She said I was just in time to apply for the fall semester, and also that I was just in time to continue as a junior. If I'd waited a year and a half longer, I would have had to start from scratch! She gave me a thick application I would have to complete at home, saying I could return it in person or mail it in. I wanted to fill it out then and there, but didn't have all the required info. We chatted a few minutes more and I took off.

Going back down the stairs, I felt a sense of relief and new beginnings, the way Joe Buck, in the film "Midnight Cowboy," must have felt when he got off the bus in Florida, leaving dead Rico alone in the seat just long enough to trade his hustler's western-style fringed leather coat, cowboy hat and boots for some nondescript slacks and a short-sleeved shirt. I was back at the admissions office two days later to return the application. The same woman was there, and she remembered me. I handed her the paperwork and she wished me luck.

Bobby Love World Tour

Seeing as how the club circuit was so limited, Bobby and Lee had recently been playing with the idea of concerts, like the show in Atchison, only on a grander scale. Kind of.

The idea was, if Bobby could fill a hall at, say, five dollars a head, he could make a lot more money than doing bar gigs. Basically, it was good thinking. The Love Machine liked it because there wouldn't be any dance sets to play. Just a warm-up and two shows, or one long show, depending. By the end of our stay at the Monroe, Bobby was ready and the big concert tour set to go. Maybe things were looking up.

But remember, Lee Miller had a heavy hand in this.

It was a great itinerary. Four cities – count 'em! – in one week: Chillicothe! Waverly! Slater! Braymer! All in Missouri, within a hundred miles of each other.

We had Sunday and Monday off, and Tuesday we were off to Chillicothe.

This time, though, we weren't playing Duke's.

We had two concerts at the American Legion Hall, Tuesday and Wednesday. Bobby had given us the address in advance, and, as usual, would meet us there with Hollywood.

We didn't remember seeing the American Legion Hall the last time in Chillicothe. No doubt we had passed it several times.

Once again, we drove clear through town on Highway 65, and missed it. We pulled over in the grocery store parking lot, the store we had grown so fond of the last time we were in town.

"That couldn't have been it that we passed by the Caterpillar place, could it?" asked Bob.

"Ha. Probably," said Barry.

We had passed a little stone building on the west side of the road, on the block where the hall should have been, but none of us believed that little building could have been it. There was no visible address or sign marking the place.

We should have known better. There was no other place that fit the address.

"Shit. Let's turn around and go see," said Bob.

Bob pulled up to the little stone building, and he and Barry got out to look. Charles and I waited in the back of the van.

In a few seconds, we heard them laughing like fools. Charles and I looked at each other.

"This must be the place," deadpanned Charles.

"Hey, you guys," called Bob, "come out! This is it!" He and Barry laughed again. Charles and I climbed out of the van.

"Can we get in?" I asked, walking up to the door.

Sure enough, there was a metal plaque stating that this was indeed the American Legion Hall. Also, sure enough, the place was locked.

"Well, what now?" mused Charles.

"Let's look around," suggested Barry.

Although it was early afternoon, and the show didn't start until eight, we were anxious to set up as much as we could without Bobby and Hollywood and get on with it. Get to our motel, shower, relax, etc. Who could tell when someone would come to open the place up? We certainly didn't know how to get hold of them.

We wandered around hoping to find a way to sneak in. Near the back of the place, on the west wall, I found an open window within climbing reach. I jumped up and was in like Flynn.

I had entered through the kitchen window. Nothing cooking. I walked through the building, checking it out. The place was like an old lodge hall. It was empty, except for plenty of folding chairs. I went to the front door and unlocked the deadbolt. The other three were gathered back there, wondering where I was.

"Whachew boys wont?" I demanded as I flung open the door.

For a stage, there was a small, triangular riser in one corner of the main room, next to an old, upright grand piano, which was grossly out of tune.

After setting up such equipment as we had – Bob's Rhodes and Crumar, Barry's amp – we realized that one or two of us would have to stand on the floor.

Typical.

The room resembled an old schoolroom: Wooden floor, plaster walls, low ceiling. Terrible acoustics, of course.

Customarily, the club provided stage lights, the multicolored spots that lit the band during the dance sets. Bobby always had Hollywood running his spotlight wherever we worked. We didn't carry any other lighting.

But, at the hall, the only stage lighting was a single, circular, fluorescent light, hovering like a halo over the riser.

"Beam me up, Scotty," laughed Barry, looking up at the light.

We finished as best we could. Hollywood and Bobby had yet to arrive.

We went to the Sleepytime motel, same as last time, and then went to dinner in style at the Sonic.

Hollywood and Bobby finally showed up, so we went back to the hall. By show time, everything was ready but a crowd. Bob's theory was that a lot of people were still out in their fields, working. In rural Missouri, late June, it's light until after nine o'clock, daylight saving time. How could anyone get to the show by eight? Ten might be better.

Oh well. A few people did actually show up, mostly

youngsters, and old-timers, but they had a good time nonetheless.

We did our best. First, we flailed our way through a short dance set to give folks a chance to arrive. Then we beat our way through a show.

Pretty slim pickings.

After the show, Hollywood and Bobby rode off in a Ford with two women. We headed back to the motel. I called Jana. We wouldn't have a chance to visit, so we talked a while. Then The Love Machine went for dinner. Again.

Being a musician is hungry work. We cruised the town.

Nothing happening, but we did manage to find something to eat.

The next night, it was a little better. There was a group of older people, men and blue-haired women. A few of the men belonged to the legion post – they were the ones wearing their cunt caps (overseas caps). But there were more than a few young girls of the teenage persuasion. Some of them had even coerced their boyfriends to come and dance. Those girls without boyfriends had a blast dancing together or by themselves.

They were too young to remember when Elvis first came on the scene, but old enough to yearn for what he represented.

During our break between the dance set and the floor show, Barry, Bob and I headed outside for some air. The crowd stood around talking and laughing, and generally enjoying themselves, even though the punch wasn't spiked (we tried it). In one group, we overheard a big guy in overalls, about fifty, talking to his friends. He was less than enthralled.

"Aw shit, he don't look like Elvis." This time, we all heard him and saw him.

Even so, Bobby did OK that night.

We had one more night in the motel, and the next day, Thursday, we headed for Slater and the next concert in our whirlwind tour.

No hurry. Slater was less than two hours away, south of Chillicothe. We passed through Waverly, where we were playing Friday.

By mid-afternoon, we were in Slater. There was a railroad track, feed store, gas station, and, yes, a grocery store and laundromat.

A deli, too. We hadn't eaten since lunch in Chillicothe, so we were famished. The deli was the only game in town.

It sucked.

Fluorescent lights. Few tables. Wait on yourself – order at the counter. Zero atmosphere. No fries. Potato chips. The lady behind the counter was nice, and almost apologetic.

I had a tenderloin. It was mediocre and small. Not one of those elephant-ear sandwiches I was used to seeing at Zesto's back home. ("Prepared in sight, it must be right!")

I finished first, and went outside to wait for the others. It was hot, sunny and dry. In the midday heat, everything seemed more quiet than usual. Even the birds were on break. We were in downtown Slater, but it was dead. Every business but the deli was closed. For good. The old corrugated-tin grain elevator by the railroad tracks recalled days of former activity. Now, Slater looked like a ghost town. I almost expected to see tumbleweeds in the deserted street.

The old-fashioned building fronts – some black cast iron, others wood, painted white – had a far-away look, like they were standing back in time. I walked the short block down to the tracks, looked up one way and down the other. The tracks were rusty, a sign of infrequent use. Then I moved over to one of the storefronts. I reached out and touched it. It was hot in the sun. It was real. A fading town's history at my fingertips.

"Funny how old buildings have that feel."

I turned around to see Bob standing in the middle of the street behind me. He had walked up so quietly I hadn't heard him.

"Yeah," I said. I walked into the street.

A hot gust blew in from the soybean field on the other side of the tracks. We took a deep breath and gazed out across the field through the silent, shimmering heat waves.

Hollywood starting the truck snapped us out of it. We rushed back to the van, and followed him over to the high school, where we were playing.

Surprisingly, it was a large, rather modern place. The gym/auditorium was airy and the stage was wide and deep, more than sufficient for our gear and us. The gym had big windows that let in a good afternoon light and a good breeze when we opened them – there was no air conditioning. As hard as we worked during a show, it didn't matter. We always worked up a sweat no matter how low the AC was. We laughed and joked as we set up. Afterwards, we went to our nondescript motel, taking note of the nearby grocery and laundry.

First, to the store.

By now, we had roading down to an art. None of our motels, except for my room at the Sandman in Minot, had refrigerators. So we all brought coolers and certain foods that we never could find while traveling. Also, we had learned that there probably would be no restaurants or stores open after the gig, especially in the small towns where the streets rolled up early. No all-night Safeway like in Minot. And the one in Chillicothe was an aberration.

So we learned to shop early, if not often. Of course, there was no hope of heating anything up, so it was no use looking longingly at frozen pizza, which would have been a feast. Bread didn't keep well, either, and lunchmeat was out, so no late-night sandwiches for us. I got Chips Ahoy cookies, milk, smoked oysters and crackers. Charles got kipper snacks and apple juice. Barry and Bob got some other crap. Also, I had taken to bringing instant coffee, sugar and creamer along with a little electric water heater that fit in a cup for my coffee in the morning. Can't do without that java.

We all pitched in for some laundry soap too. After grocery shopping, we went to the laundry. There were days to go and no clean clothes.

Laundry is the great equalizer. One of them, at least. We got to see the locals in action. The place was busy with women and their kids. Of course, they wondered who we were, strange guys – the only guys - doing laundry in the afternoon, and we told them. Some of them knew about the concert that night, and asked about Bobby Love and things in general. So we all learned a bit about each other. It's hard not to be friendly when your socks are on the folding table.

Clothes clean, we went back to the motel, showered and got ready for the show.

Really, we wanted to go eat again, but there was no place to go. Not even a burger joint! And certainly, we weren't going back to that deli.

It was closed, anyway.

The show started at seven.

When the curtain opened, it was another teen night. Hardly any adults were present, and none we recognized from the laundromat. (Maybe we missed them.) That was OK, though, because the kids had a wild time. They danced through our opening set and screamed through Bobby's show.

Even at that, the place wasn't packed. Although we, even Bobby, had a good time playing for the kids, we could see that there weren't enough people to make it worth our while, financially, that is. But we felt good, and we did our best.

After the show, Bobby went back to the motel and we packed up the stuff with Hollywood.

The real work done, we went back to the motel ourselves. Charles and I went over to Bob and Barry's room to shoot the shit.

The next day, we got up and went over to Waverly, about thirty miles east.

Waverly is smaller than Slater, and older.

After dropping our stuff off at the motel, we went to the school, a grade school this time, to set up. We could see the school from the motel parking lot. It sat across the road, a short drive down around a curve.

This was really the "old school."

We figured it was built in the twenties. To get to the auditorium, we had to carry the stuff up two flights of steep, narrow, winding stairs. The stage was small, although complete with theatrical lights and curtains. The stage and auditorium were couched in dark wood. From the front to the back of the house, the seats (I don't think there were 200, certainly not more than 300) were arranged in a steep angle that seemed almost vertical, so they all seemed close to the stage. Overall, the place had a dark atmosphere, but not depressing.

But, oh Lord, was it ever a pain lugging all that equipment up those stairs. And we were all too aware that we would have to lug it right back down.

We set up and did a sound check. The auditorium was small enough that we couldn't play too loud, but the acoustics were good. After that, we explored the place.

We strolled the halls and peered in some classrooms. Desks were all in a row, there were books on the shelves, the blackboards were clean. There's a certain feel and smell to old schools when they're closed and empty for the summer. The air had that mustiness that comes from chalk dust, books and closed windows.

Another great afternoon at a motel, the most crummy one to date. It wasn't dirty, just old and tired. Somehow, we found a burger joint where we could eat. Unfortunately, we didn't get a chance to find a grocery.

We got to the school about seven-thirty, and geared up

for the eight-o'clock show.

If Bobby had any doubts, he didn't let on. The rest of us, though, were skeptical. How could Bobby draw enough people to fill this place? It wouldn't take many to pack the house. But who was gonna show up? Waverly was a long way from Vegas.

Our recurrent nightmare and running joke was the curtain opening on an empty house.

Not quite, this time. The curtain rose on about thirty fans, mostly teenage girls again. They made a small but vigorous audience, running down to stand at the stage apron and ogle Bobby. He gave out scarves to each girl and some of their mothers. They loved it.

We were done by ten, hurriedly packed up our gear, practically threw it down the narrow stairs, and retreated to the motel to regroup.

"I'm hungry," said Barry.

"Me too," answered Bob. "Let's go see what we can find."

We piled into the van and headed down the dark road. Hollywood and Bobby had already crashed, amazingly. They, too, were road-worn, and there were no parties to be found.

We drove around for almost an hour. First, we went down the belt highway. Surely a main road would have someplace to eat.

No.

We drove back the other direction. No luck.

Barry fired up a joint, and we headed for a promising group of lights that seemed close to the horizon. It took about twenty minutes to reach them.

Gas stations, but no food.

Somehow, we made our way into the heart of Waverly, but we could see that the streets had been long since rolled up. We passed a 7-Eleven, but we were looking for a real place to eat. It wasn't gonna happen.

"Well," said Bob dejectedly, "looks like the seven-eleven."

Although they had a microwave, frozen pizza was out of the question. The oven wasn't big enough. Bob got a burger, Charles made sure to get something without pork in it – a beef sandwich. I got a sleazy burrito, and Barry got a Junkyard Dog, a hot dog with cheese and other shit on it.

As we ate in the van in front of the 7-Eleven store, we laughed at our food. Luckily, I still had some milk and cookies in the cooler back at the motel.

To break the routine, Charles and Barry shared a room, and Bob and I shared one. We had a good time listening to tapes, talking and philosophizing.

As we readied for bed, we were distracted by four flies buzzing the room. We both swatted at them determinedly. No luck.

"Damned flies," groused Bob.

"Yeah," I said, "maybe I can get 'em."

I stalked the flies. I could tell they had landed when the buzzing stopped. They were on the ceiling. But I didn't have anything to swat them with – no newspaper or magazine.

In every motel room, though, is a Gideon Bible. I took it out of the little nightstand drawer. In a burst of blasphemy, I used it to smash the flies on the ceiling, right to the Armstrong acoustic tile.

Only one got away, and it was in hiding. Now the room was quiet enough to get some sleep.

Besides, it was something to do.

Next day, we landed in Braymer.

Braymer is even smaller than Waverly. Only about 60 miles from Kansas City, it might as well have been on another planet.

It was Saturday, and since this was the last stop on the tour, we had no plans to stay the night. After the show, we would head home.

The concert was at a combination bar and roller rink. It was one of those places where everyone brings their own booze, and then buys the mixers – usually pop, tonic water, club soda and ice – at the club's store. "Setups," they call it. Indeed.

We pulled into town hungry. The only place open was a dinky burger joint, smaller than the deli in Slater. There didn't seem to be any other restaurants in town here, either. Well, there was one, but it was a breakfast spot that closed at two p.m. We got there at three.

The burger joint was crowded with locals, but we found a table and then went to order from the counter. No waitresses here, either. At least the food was better than Slater's. They made real burgers and fries and did a good job of it.

After eating, we found our way to the club. It was a new building outside of town on a winding road. There was no missing it. It was the only place around the place. We were set up by five p.m. There was nothing to do but play ball in the lot. The show started at eight.

By six-thirty, people started arriving. They all knew each other, and there was the feel of a social gathering. It looked like there would be a good crowd. This time the adults outnumbered the kids. Some of them were dressed as if they were going to a square dance. But there was still a good number of younger folks, mainly the ubiquitous teenage girls.

On time, at eight, we took the stage and began our dance set. The stage was quite large, which we much appreciated, and elevated off the roller fink floor about five feet. It, like the stage at the Monroe Inn, had a wooden railing around it that made it feel like a corral.

Although none of our dance songs were country, the people responded well. Folks of all ages were bumping and hopping to the sounds of The Love Machine.

At the end of our set, a very large man resembling Junior

Samples (from the TV show Hee-Haw) asked if he could use the mike to make an announcement. It was for a contest or something. That was OK with us.

After that, though, he wanted us to back him while he sang a song. It was one thing to make an announcement, but we weren't going to back him on a song. What was this, amateur night? Open-mike night? When we heard him ask Bob about backing him, Charles, Barry and I quickly took the back stairs off the stage and melted into the crowd like we never heard him. There was nothing for Bob to do but politely refuse. "The band's already gone on break," as he later reported to us. "Boy," he told us later, "was I glad you guys split."

All of us were glad that this was our last gig for the week.

"Boy m' boy!" exclaimed Bobby jovially, before the next set. "I can't wait to get home and do laundry. I'm on my cleanest pair of dirty pants!"

To brighten our day, Connie showed up with members of the fan club. She had missed Slater, but no one faulted her for that.

For this show, we played dance sets before the first and second acts. They were only half-hour sets, nothing to it. And, we got to mingle with the crowd some. This was something we didn't particularly like or excel at, but which Bobby wanted us to do.

Some girls asked us to autograph their Bobby Love souvenir photos, and we happily obliged. How could we not? They were so giggly and happy talking to us. I was so road-worn that I almost signed my real name, instead of Frankie Stone. I recovered quickly and corrected. No use confusing the fans and blowing the cover and image! The girls were thrilled.

The show closed, we packed up and went home. Hurry though we might, it was two a.m. Sunday morning when I walked in the door.

The first thing I noticed was that the dishes from last

Monday, and those of the week, were still in the sink, unwashed.

Sunday afternoon, I did the dishes. They had a week's worth of gross on them from sitting in the water. Later, I asked Anne why she hadn't done them.

Not that I thought it was her duty. I have no problem doing dishes, no question. This is especially true after my experience with commune living, where it was all too common to walk into the kitchen and see a mountain of dirty dishes. Every last dish in the house would be in a festering heap, making it necessary to wash a glass even for a drink of water. Jeez! But it wasn't like Anne to leave dishes stewing in the sink all week.

"Oh, I just didn't get around to doing them. Anita and I got together a few times, and I was tired from work."

I didn't argue. I believed her. Anita was a good friend of ours who also worked for the city. Still, I could tell something was amiss. We had a short, quiet weekend.

Monday, we were playing at the Blue Springs, Missouri, civic center. Another concert week. Slated to be a bigger week yet, we had a concert every night in different towns, if not bigger. It was exciting. At least, Bobby and Lee were excited. Even we almost began to think that the Bobby Love Show might actually take off. If the concerts went all right, we all stood to make some good money. Depending on attendance, we could have made more than double union scale, which was $32 a night for sidemen. (I never knew what Bobby made, but as bandleader he would get the lion's share.)

It was a sticky ninety-five degrees as I hit I-70 for Blue Springs, twenty miles east of Kansas City. We were supposed to meet there at five-thirty, and the concert began at eight.

The civic center was easy to find. I got there about five-fifteen. There was no sign of the others.

I waited.

By six, they still weren't there and I was hungry. Patricio's Mexican restaurant was nearby, and I went to eat.

Mmmmm, tacos.

It was almost seven when I got back, and everyone was there, and damned near set up.

"Well, thought you'd show up, huh?" cracked Bob sarcastically.

"Think we're roadies?" chimed in Charles.

"Just fuck you guys," I bristled. "I've been here since five-fifteen, and went to eat about six."

"I bet," continued Bob. "We got here about six."

"Then I must've just missed you. Besides, we were supposed to be here by five-thirty."

They helped me carry in my equipment, and that was that. Case closed.

After setting up, we went to the dressing room.

Even better than the Atchison Armory, the civic center was a new, modern facility, and we had a real dressing room. Carpeted, air-conditioned. It was great. No cases of liquor to step around or mop buckets to step in.

Connie and Janine were sitting on the carpet using scissors to cut out scarves of varying colors. There could be no show without the scarves. And the kisses.

"Having fun, Connie?" I teased.

"Oh, just loads," she quipped, jumping up to give us all a hug.

Just for the hell of it, we took some souvenir scarves for ourselves. As a reminder. Of course, we didn't have to kiss Bobby. Anywhere.

When Connie and Janine were finished, Hollywood Bob rounded up the scarves, hung them on the mike stand he always used for a rack and took them to the stage. By the time Bobby and Lee Miller breezed into the dressing room, we were suited up and ready to go.

"Hi guys," Bobby greeted cheerfully. "Ready to go knock 'em out tonight?"

"Yeah, if they show up," said Bob.

"Aw, they'll show up," said Bobby, disappointed by Bob's gloomy tone. "I mean, we 'four-walled' this sucker."

From our blank stares, it was clear to Bobby that we had no idea what "four-walling" meant.

"You know," he explained, "I got ads on TV, radio, newspaper, flyers out. We're doing our best to get the word out on the show."

"Well, I hope it works," said Charles.

"I think it'll be OK," said Lee. "We're gonna try to get this place tomorrow night, too."

"But what about Slater and Marshall, and wherever?" asked Barry, referring to the concerts planned for the rest of the week.

"Well," drawled Lee, "they canceled."

"What?" we all cried in unified alarm.

"They canceled, except for Polo."

"I thought we had contracts," Charles moaned.

"Well, we did too," excused Lee. "But they canceled at the last minute. But, we still have the Polo gig on Thursday, and Warrensburg Friday and Saturday."

"Great," I muttered. I could see dollar signs flying away from me at a rapid rate. Faster than galaxies in the ever-expanding universe.

With mixed feelings, we took the stage, hidden from the audience by the drawn curtain.

The stage was excellent. Roomy, modern, good lighting, it had built-in spotlights with color gels, and Hollywood had a real booth from which to run his spotlight.

Bobby was charging six dollars admission, children under twelve free. There was a big poster in the foyer.

Still we were nervous. What would we see when the curtain opened?

It was time. In lieu of a dance set we would play a warm-up set, since there was no place to dance.

As we kicked off our first number, the curtain opened – to reveal less than a hundred people. Not even enough to fill the first five rows. As we played, we looked at each other. It was hard not to laugh. Crying on stage is not allowed.

"Pretty thin out there," noted Charles between songs.

It was a small audience but vocal. They loved our opener. And they were ready for Bobby. The fifties segment covering Elvis' early years was really a hit. We took a brief intermission before the second act and went backstage.

"Where is everybody?" wondered Barry, "I mean, what's there to do in Blue Springs?"

"Well," mused Bob, "I think David Cassidy's at Starlight Theater tonight, and the Yardbirds are having a reunion concert at Memorial Hall. I mean, there's some stiff competition."

"Besides," I threw in, "who'd want to pay six dollars to see Bobby Love, when, for a dollar more, they could see a real concert?"

The Love Machine returned to play some more tunes, keeping everyone's attention while Bobby finished a costume change. When he was ready, we stopped playing, the curtain closed, and the house lights went down.

The 2001 theme rumbled through the hall as the curtain opened. We moved into Viva Las Vegas and Bobby took the stage. Elvis' comeback concert in Las Vegas, 1969, was on. It was a solid performance. The crowd loved it and, in typical fashion, mobbed the stage apron, moms, teenage girls and kids alike. It was frustrating to be so well received and have such a small audience.

Bobby and Lee decided to try it another night. Why not? The hall was available, and we had no other place to play until Friday, except for Polo.

During the sound check before Tuesday's show, my amp wouldn't work. Horror of horrors. Truly a worst-case scenario. It had worked fine the night before. I was panic-stricken, even though I could have run through the PA if it got down to it. Luckily, Hollywood always had his amp head with him. He had an Acoustic bass amp. Those had good power and tone. Hollywood always brought it along for just such an emergency. A good Scout. What a relief. I would have to take my amp head to be fixed, and Hollywood said I could use his while I waited.

Four-walling notwithstanding, again the curtain opened on a nearly empty house. We said good-bye to Blue Springs, sat out Wednesday, and got ready for Polo and our weekend in Warrensburg.

On Thursday, we made the trip to Polo, Missouri, a town of less than six hundred at the junction of highways 13 and 116, just a few miles east of Braymer. It was an out-and-back. No motel. Go play and come home. A one-day concert tour. It went fine. Seems like we played a barn, but it may have been another roller rink. Maybe it was a combination. I had my eyes closed.

On Friday, we headed to Warrensburg, a small town about sixty miles east of Kansas City. Home to Central Missouri State University, it sits in the middle of farm country. In July there wouldn't be much college action, but Warrensburg was the biggest town we'd played in a while. We were almost excited about it.

The place we were playing had nothing to do with the university, although Bobby probably could have done well during the school season. We were playing in a roller rink that served as a bar and dance hall. Yes, another one. And this one also worked on the setup method.

It was huge. So big, we could play Frisbee and not throw

the damned thing from one end to the other. So big, I swear I saw the curve of the earth.

Happily, it was fairly new and clean. The rink proper was an oval with a concrete floor painted a nice, shiny light gray, enclosed by a cinder-block wall about four feet high to keep skaters from flying into the seats. On the far side of the rink, opposite the entrance, there was a stage that folded against the back wall, sort of a giant Murphy bed. But it was a big stage with plenty of room. We lowered it and set up the equipment.

Bobby had an office to use for his dressing room, so he could enter the arena from behind the stage. We, however, had to use the rest rooms. When the time came to change, we had Connie, omnipresent, faithful Connie, guard the door for us.

"No peeking," Barry teased her.

While waiting for show time, Barry hatched a plan.

This was the year of the Unknown Comic, a stand-up comedian who performed with a paper bag over his head (the bag had eye and mouth holes cut out), and a small bag (also with cutouts) for a hand puppet.

"Why don't we," said Barry conspiratorially, "put bags on our heads and be the Unknown Band?"

We cracked up. "Don't tempt me," laughed Bob.

"We are the Unknown Band!" I observed, still laughing.

It seemed too good to pass up, but we figured Bobby would shoot us if we did. Besides, none of us had any bags.

"Well," suggested Charles, "how about sunglasses?"

"Yeah! Great!" Of course! We all had shades.

We opened with our usual dance set. Even before we started, there was a full crowd. Quite a nice change from the concerts so far. If the crowd looked small, it was because the room was so big.

At the end of the set, Patsy and Denise came up to the stage and greeted us. Patsy had our photos, just as she had promised back in Poplar Bluff. She gave each of us an envelope with four snapshots. I got an individual shot, the wacky stage pose, and two random shots. On the back of one of my photos – I'm sure she did the same for the others – she noted, in the nicest handwriting you can imagine, my name, the date and location taken. She signed it, "Patsy Sylvester, Sweet Springs, Missouri."

After a short break, it was time for Bobby's first show. The fifties.

We looked at each other and donned our shades.

Bobby took the floor to much applause, and broke right into Shake, Rattle, And Roll. Bobby was hot – the crowd was thrilled. He was well into the third song before he happened to turn around.

It took about half a beat to register. He did a double take.

If looks could kill.

Then he got the joke and laughed, and we laughed, and carried on.

Even blinded by Hollywood's spotlight, we could see that the place was crowded. Most of the tables around the rink were full. They had even put tables on the rink itself, and there was a crush of people surrounding Bobby on the floor. The bodyguards had their hands full.

One disadvantage of not having a stage was that fans could crowd in and cramp Bobby's style. The band would be on the stage and Bobby would perform on the dance floor in most situations. Hence, floor show. The bodyguards did their best to establish a perimeter, but the ladies pressed in close.

The audience loved Bobby in his gold lamé suit, and even in the cavernous expanse of the roller rink the sound was good. Lord knows we had enough equipment to make sure everyone in Warrensburg could hear us.

After the set, Bobby didn't mention the glasses routine. I think he was getting used to us but thought of us as offbeat weirdos. And he could handle that as long as we played like smokin' sons-of-bitches on stage.

During the break between shows, all the band members were sitting at a table by the wall, having a drink. (We'd brought our own.) Connie came up to us and said that a reporter from the KC Scene, a Kansas City entertainment paper, was here to interview Bobby, and would like to talk to us too.

Gee, we were excited. The press wanted to talk to us.

Then it hit us, and we got nervous. What could we say about the show? About Bobby? About our so-called career intentions?

"Bob, you're the leader, you talk to her first," decided Charles.

The reporter's name was Joyce. She was not a threatening figure. Joyce was about our age, wore jeans and a blouse rather than a suit, and didn't even carry a tape recorder. She could have, should have, sat and had a drink with us. As Bob and Joyce sat down to talk at another table, she whipped out her notebook.

"How," she began, "did you get involved with the Bobby Love Show?"

Bob thought a minute. "Well, for me, it was a career move. I'd been on the road for two years with another show band, and was looking for something a little more exciting." This was becoming Bob's standard explanation.

"You find Bobby's show exciting?"

He laughed. "Oh, yes. Very." Bob looked over at us, grinning.

"Do you think Bobby will be successful?"

"Yes, if he keeps working at the show, improving it, and works toward a more professional venue, like Vegas."

"Would you like to play Vegas?"

"Sure! I played there when I was with the Tommy Riggs Show, and it was an interesting place. And the money's good."

"Does Bobby run the show by himself, or does he listen to his band members? I guess I mean, what do you think are your contributions to the show?"

"It's definitely Bobby's show. He planned and choreographed it. But he listens to what we have to say, musically. Our – the band's – main interest, I feel, is to present a quality act. And we work hard at this. It's this idea of quality that everyone in the band is committed to, and it's quality that's important to us." Bob went on to explain his theory of quality and its relation to "Zen and the Art of Motorcycle Maintenance."

From time to time, as Bob and Joyce talked, the rest of us would glance at each other and stifle a laugh. But we knew our turn was coming.

Joyce talked to each of us, but not as long as she talked to Bob. From us, she got vital statistics, basic desires and goals.

Charles, for instance, was interested in continuing his show business career, but not necessarily as a drummer. Eventually, he wanted his own show.

I, for my part, was going to use music as a means to work my way through school, and start a career in writing. Or careening in writing.

"So," Joyce asked me, "you don't see music as a permanent way of life?"

"No."

"Really?"

"You know," I elaborated, "there's not much security in it, and a person could play bars until old age and not have anything to show for it. No vacation, or paid sick leave. Fewer benefits than being a reporter." Joyce laughed and nodded knowingly.

I figured not much of this would get into print. When I saw her story in the Scene a couple of weeks later, Joyce had done all right by us.

By now, it was show time. Viva Las Vegas! I bid Joyce

adieu and joined the others on stage.

This night, Bobby wore his red jumpsuit.

Hot-cha! Look out!

Saturday night we were ready again. We all got down there early so we could eat together. The band, that is. Anne came with me, and Debbie came with Barry. Charles and Bob were solo. There was a party atmosphere during our dinner at a pizza joint. Happily fed, we headed for the roller rink.

No sunglasses stunts tonight. By and large, it was a solid, satisfying show, and we had a good crowd, although not like the night before. That seems so typical of clubs on weekends. One night will be killer, the other just crowded. But it's hard to predict which night it will be. Sometimes Friday, other times Saturday. Just one of those mysteries.

Of course, Connie was there with other fan club members. So were Ed and Willa.

How Ed got into the music business is another mystery. He owned a machine shop in Independence, Missouri, and seemed quite successful at it. Maybe it was a vicarious thing, maybe a way to make more money (can't see that, though).

Willa was willowy and good-looking, with short, curly, brown hair. She also seemed to have a good sense of humor. Maybe it was Willa that got Ed into this circus. She really liked the show, and all of us in the band. Bob and Barry always half-jokingly said that Willa had the hots for the band, and that might have been true. I think Willa just wanted to be in on the fun. She and Ed often brought their two boys, who were about eight and nine, to see the show.

Ed often showed up when we were close to Kansas City. Partly to check on the show, and partly to pay us in person. He liked the band members and wanted to make sure everything was going well for us.

The show was over, the equipment packed. Anne and I were sitting at a table with Charles, Barry and Debbie, inside the rink against the wall. Ed, the club owner, and a small crowd of hangers-on were standing across the room near the front door.

Pretty soon it dawned on us that we had been talking for quite a while, about forty-five minutes. We had seen Ed walk out the front door, and return a few minutes later. But, we were far enough away that we couldn't tell if there was a fight or not outside the door. It wasn't like Ed to keep us waiting for the money.

"Charles, what do you think?" I asked.

"I think I'll go ask Bobby or Ed what's going on."

He came back shortly. Too shortly.

"Ed says there's a woman with a gun who's stolen the check. He's trying to get it back."

When Charles mentioned a gun, we all hunched lower at the table, and were glad to be behind the rink's cinder-block wall.

"Gun?" I asked. "Barry, where's your two friends?"

"I've got my Ruger," he assured us.

Suddenly, there was a definite commotion at the front door. The owner, a fiftyish, balding man, had gone outside to try and catch the woman. Ed went out again too.

We tried to look while keeping our heads low, in case of flying lead. When Ed walked out, he had his right hand in the pocket of his sport coat.

Soon, Ed came back with the check. He paid us. There'd been no shooting.

We never did get the whole story about how the woman came to get our check. It seems she had some argument with the owner, a running feud. Evidently, Bobby had nothing directly to do with it, except to get caught in the middle. Innocent, for once.

Ed also informed us that beginning Monday, we would be at a joint called the Balcony, out in Edwardsville, Kansas. This was a home game, since it was close enough to drive to every night.

Road or not, we were relieved to have a steady gig. These concerts had turned out to be a bust.

Performance-wise, they were fine. Easy work, save for moving equipment more often. But they didn't have the effect that Bobby and Lee thought they would. Namely, putting the Bobby Love Show on the map.

Final Curtain

THE BALCONY WAS OUT AT 98TH and Kaw Drive in Edwardsville, a suburb west of Kansas City, Kansas, a good half-hour drive from my house. The club was on the south side of a lonely stretch of two-lane highway. Across the road from the place sat the nearest outpost of civilization, a defunct gas station. A railroad track paralleled Kaw Drive less than three hundred feet behind the Balcony. Whenever a train roared by, it felt like we were in a cocktail shaker.

The show opened at eight-thirty Monday night. Everyone but Bobby – Bob, Barry, Hollywood, Charles and I – got there late in the afternoon to set up. The Balcony looked like a nondescript, oblong one-story whitewashed brick building. Next to the door, the standard neon beer signs for Bud and Oly glowed in the only window. We went in to scout out the joint. Outside, the July sun cast a glaring hot light. Inside it was dark as a tomb.

Once our eyes adjusted, we could see we were on the upper floor, which really was a balcony extending along three walls.

The bar and two small offices, which would double as our dressing rooms, were along the wall to our left. A scattering of small cocktail tables had a good view of the stage and floor below. Along the back wall a steep, narrow stairway, with no railing, descended about twenty feet.

To our right, more cocktail tables sat along a wrought-iron fence that wrapped around to the far wall. Walking this narrower balcony could be tricky in the dim lighting. One misstep and busy waitresses, woozy customers, and band members could tumble onto the tables below, just like stuntmen in the Westerns.

The balcony connected an old-fashioned, iron spiral staircase leading down to the lower floor, next to the bandstand in the corner. Douglas Fairbanks would have loved it – from the spiral stairs to the stage in one leap! Too bad there wasn't a rope to swing on for us to make an entrance.

The spiral stairs looked cool, but there was no way to carry any of our amps and stuff down the spiral stairs, so we lugged it all down the steep stairway along the back. While setting up our gear, we looked up along the three sides of the balcony. A few early drinkers were looking back down at us.

"Damn," said Barry. "It's more like the pit than the balcony."

To top it off, the Balcony seemed to be one of those shoot-your-way-in-and-out kinds of places. One of the local patrons filled us in as we carried the equipment.

"Oh, it's OK. You know, we dance a dance, then we fight a dance, then we dance a dance, and so on," he said happily.

The hours were eight-thirty p.m. to two a.m. This was an extra hour and a half, compared to the usual to nine to one. And for no extra money.

All in all, it turned out the Balcony's patrons were regular folks, lively enough, and we didn't see any fights. The Bobby Love Show was a real hit with them. They even took it in good stride whenever a train would barrel past on the tracks behind the place, shaking, rattling and rolling the building. And if the train whistle blew, that pretty much drowned out the show. It happened at least twice a night.

No doubt about it, though, Bobby Love and the Love Machine were hot. As a band, the Love Machine was zeroed in and Bobby made the most of it. He played off us, we played off him. Keeping the basic framework – early Elvis and Vegas Elvis – we could change song order or add material at will, vamp, and improvise as needed. Sometimes it was fast and loose, but the excitement galvanized the crowd. And Bobby had grown to like us as a band, even though he still wasn't sure what to make of us personally. He still saw us as eccentric musicians. Sparse as he was with compliments, we could tell he was actually rather proud of us.

If he didn't compliment much, he complained even less. But the winds of discontent were blowing, and we were getting a little cynical about the whole thing.

For one, it was becoming obvious that no matter how much better we got, we would never play any better joints. Clubs with class and money. Especially money. There would be no Vegas, let alone Europe or Japan, for chrissake.

Not that we couldn't have carried it off. We were good and getting better all the time. And there was a demand for such acts. Some, like Alan, another Elvis impersonator, were playing Vegas for big money and putting albums out. An album of Elvis songs played by a guy imitating Elvis. And, to an extent, it was selling. So, yes, while there was a market for Bobby's act, we would have to strike while the iron was hot. Ride the wave. Make a bundle while the makin' is good and get out.

Although none of us ever mentioned it, we hadn't forgotten about the Chillicothe incident. And we still felt it was small-time, inept management, fouling up the bookings. Of course, we realized that sometimes you have to take what you can get. But still, we all, including Hollywood, felt that a little more class – with a capital C – on the management end would have helped. We felt dead-ended and jaded.

More critical, just how far could we expect to go with an act that was essentially, as Bob had put it, grave robbing? We still felt Bobby could have put together a dynamite nightclub act, drawing material from a number of sources. Hell, in the previous year or so he had been doing a Tom Jones tribute, of all things. But he seemed stuck on Elvis, and there was no convincing him. And, of course, he had invested a small fortune in costumes and the wig, parted on the wrong side or not. Might as well get some use out of them.

I was thinking of bailing out, and so was Bob. But it was confusing. Working in a band was what I had wanted. Or so I had thought. Now it was turning out to be just work, like any other job.

I felt guilty about wanting to quit so soon. Things had just gotten started. I was too proud to try and go back to my job at the City. Besides, they'd already filled the position. And I was waiting to hear the verdict on my application to UMKC. So, it looked as if I would carry on for a while.

All the Love Machine members came to the club dressed for the show. As usual, there was no real dressing room. Bobby used one of the manager's offices. We could have dressed there, too, but we passed. It was easier just to show up ready to go.

Charles was riding with me during this gig. He drove to my house, and I would take it from there. The company was good. All of us tried to leave home as late as possible so we wouldn't have to hang around the club. Although air-conditioned, it was not the greatest place for socializing. Even less attractive was standing around outside in the heat, sweating in our tuxes.

A few times we got there early enough to share a drink and a joint (excluding Charles) before show time. Get "gheed up," as Bob put it. Often Hollywood would join us or invite us to smoke one of his. Bobby would have liked us to get there earlier to mingle with the crowd, but we weren't into it. Oh, we'd stop between sets and shoot the shit if someone called to us, and we were on good terms with the bartenders and waitresses. It irritated Bobby that we didn't socialize more, but what the hell.

Even so, the crowd liked us. If we didn't mingle, we didn't insult them, either. We were always gracious to a fault. Every now and then, someone would take a liking to us and send up a round.

By this time, all of us, except Charles, had taken to drinking straight shots of Black Jack – Jack Daniels Black Label. Barry got us started on that. We liked the idea because shots wouldn't water down with melted ice during the set. Charles stuck to his orange juice.

So whenever the waitress, usually Shirley, asked what we were drinking, it was always three shots, one orange juice.

One night, though, something just got lost in the translation.

All night.

It started during the first set. Shirley brought us four shots, no juice. Charles told her, nicely, that he wanted juice.

It never came. The rest of us – Bob, Barry, and myself – drank up, leaving one shot left.

Not long after, another round showed up. Four shots. Poor Charles was getting frustrated and thirsty. On break he went to get his own damn juice.

Next set, same thing. We got a round about every twenty minutes all night. With Charles not drinking, that meant that every third round we had a bonus round.

By the end of the night we were reeling.

"Can you drive?" one of the waitresses asked Bob, seeing his condition.

"Gotta drive. Too drunk to walk."

As we closed the last set, we got one more round.

"We're gonna die, Shirley," stammered Barry.

"Take 'em back," pleaded Bob.

"I can't," she said, smiling sweetly, leaving the tray on the stage.

We looked at each other. Barry had an idea. "Let's hide

'em in the tool box for tomorrow night."

The next night, before our first set, we opened the toolbox. There they sat. Four shots. We each downed one and, in honor of Charles, passed around the fourth. It was a good night.

This same night, something happened that I had been expecting all along.

All this time, it will be recalled, Bobby had been introducing the band as "Bob Buster, from Las Vegas, Nevada; Barry Johnson, from Woodbridge, New Jersey; Frankie Stone, from Newport News, Virginia; and the spark plug of the Love Machine, Charles Sharrieff, from San Bernardino, California."

This, of course, added to the show's overarching glamour.

After the last show of the night, during our break before our dance set, Shirley came up to me and said that there was somebody that wanted to meet me. She pointed to a group of three couples under the balcony, not far from the stage. They waved as I looked over.

"Hello," I said, approaching the table.

"Hello," said a woman, standing to shake my hand. She was probably in her forties. "So," she went on, sitting back down, "you're from Newport News?"

I almost choked. "Why sure!" I said, remembering the woman in Chillicothe.

"Me too," said the woman.

I just knew she was going to ask me what high school I went to, or what part of town I was from. Quickly, I was dreaming up lies. The only thing I knew about Newport News was that it's on the coast of Virginia.

"Have you been there recently?" she asked.

"No, ma'am. I've been gone a long time," I storied, implying a quick move after birth.

"Well, we like your show very much, and it's good to see someone from home," she finished, shaking my hand again.

I nodded, smiling, and managed to edge off before old times came up.

Nothing could change the dissatisfaction brewing in all of us, and me especially.

For my part, I was frustrated by a home life that wasn't there, and by the demands of a musical career that had no traction.

Long before I had joined the Bobby Love Show, Anne had planned our almost-annual trip to see her aunt and uncle in Biloxi, Mississippi. Aunt Jane taught school and Uncle Red ran a charter fishing boat. He would sometimes take us out fishing in the Gulf. Jane was also one of the few women in the Gulf to earn a pilot's license. Pilots steer ships from the Gulf to the harbor in New Orleans. Passing the pilot test was simple, as Red described it. "All you have to do is memorize the Mississippi River and draw a map of it, noting all the hazards."

Sure, it was grippingly humid in Biloxi, but still it was fun to visit. The Gulf Coast is more relaxed compared to the rest of Mississippi.

Even so, sometimes we were reminded this was still the South, as I learned one time when Aunt Jane took us to breakfast at a local restaurant.

I ordered eggs, bacon, hash browns. No grits. Eggs over easy.

"You want biscuits or toast?" asked the waitress.

I thought about it a second. "Toast," out of habit.

"So, a Yankee huh?" she said, grinning.

The food was great.

We knew when I joined the show that our vacation plans might get messed up. That's show biz. We had already missed seeing "A Chorus Line" when it came to town. Rather, I missed it. We had bought tickets long before I joined the show, so

Anne took Anita. Neither Anne nor I tried to think about it. But here it was summer, and the trip was looming. Even more so because things weren't going so well between us. Anne decided she was going with or without me, which didn't make me feel any better about the situation.

Myself, I was ready for a vacation. Maybe, I figured, it would help my marriage, and cool some of the craziness of working in music. Ed Frazier was going to be at the Balcony that Friday, and I determined to talk to him.

It wasn't easy. Musicians just don't get vacations unless everyone gets one. The problem is obvious. Who would fill in? Could I come back? Would I?

Ed and Bobby weren't all that pleased, but they weren't angry, either. I explained the situation, and they agreed that maybe I needed some time off. They had two weeks to find a fill-in, and felt sure it could be done.

I felt better, but still nervous.

The next night, Saturday, as Charles and I walked into the Balcony, Lee Miller was there to greet us.

"Charles, Frank, this is our last n-night here."

Charles and I looked at each other.

"I thought we had another week," I said.

"W-well," stuttered Lee, "Bobby had a d-death in the family – his f-f-father – and he had to take off to go to the funeral."

We were stunned.

"What about the show tonight?" asked Charles.

"You guys will have to p-play tonight without Bobby," said Lee with downcast eyes.

Aarrrgghh! That meant no show and a whole night playing dance music.

"That's sad," lamented Charles.

"Yeah," I said. "Even a guy like Bobby has to have a dad, I guess."

We went into the dressing room. Bob was already there.

"So, did Lee tell you two the news?"

"Yeah."

All of Bobby's stuff – costumes, makeup, everything – was gone. Not a trace. Not even empty bottles.

That it might be a ruse never occurred to us. That there might have been an argument or disagreement with the club owner was the farthest thing from our minds. Now it started to look fishy.

"What are we gonna do next week?" asked Charles.

"I'm not sure," said Bob. "Lee said he or Ed would tell us tomorrow or Monday. Maybe Genova's." None of us had come prepared. As far as we knew, we had another week at the Balcony. We would have to break the equipment down in our tuxes. Great. The world's best-dressed roadies.

"Ladies and gentlemen," began Charles, "before we begin tonight, we have an announcement. Due to a death in the family, Bobby Love will not be able to appear tonight. His father has died, and he had to leave town for the funeral." Yeah, leave town.

An audible groan arose from the crowd. Charles continued.

"But, ladies and gentlemen, the show must go on, and the Love Machine will play for your dancing pleasure tonight, as scheduled." With that, we launched into 2001 to start our show.

That was the night my own dad had finally come to see the show. And no damn Bobby.

It was a long night without Bobby Love. Sort of like Poplar Bluff, but with a full house. As usual, though, we toughed our way through, and Hollywood played the spotlight on us. He had to do something. We all – band and crowd – made the best of it, and had fun.

And then it was over. We tore down and packed up the

equipment after Ed paid us. It was raining when we left.

Monday afternoon, Lee Miller called and told all of us to be down at Genova's that evening.

We converged about five-thirty. It was old home week all over again. There was Pete, and Joe, and old Mr. Charlie. Gosh.

We set up in leisurely fashion. The show didn't start until Tuesday, and Bobby was still "out of town."

By now, I was pretty certain that my vacation would be a permanent one. To be sure, the weird craziness surrounding the show had a lot to do with it. But now, I had another reason. I had heard from UMKC and had been accepted as a junior, just as I expected. It was thrilling. When I told Charles, he grinned and slapped me on the back.

"Man, I knew you could do it."

When Bobby showed up at Genova's Tuesday, we all gave our condolences.

"Yeah, well," he said, "these things happen. We all gotta go sometime. Thanks, guys." He seemed a little surprised that we would show concern. Maybe he was surprised that we seemed to believe him. We were hedging our bets just in case.

Genova's was full, but not packed. Not humming. Was Bobby wearing out his welcome? We would have to wait for the weekend to be sure. At least, Genova's always had good advertising. Not all clubs did. Many owners expected the act to carry it alone, and then bitched about poor turnouts.

Later that night, I talked to Bobby, telling him that I had been accepted at the university. I wanted to be sure about his plans to travel. It might make a difference regarding whether I stayed with the show. Bobby was still adamant about the road, saying that we had to travel to keep working. He was right about that. I was torn, and wanted to stay with the group, but it would be hard to be in school and on the road at the same time. Bobby lost the toss.

Bob had also decided to throw in the towel.

"I can't take it anymore," he said during a break. "I gotta get something more respectable. Steady. It's like you said, Frank. A guy could grow old doing this and never see a thing for it. I don't want to be playing with Bobby when I'm fifty."

So. Maybe I wasn't totally off the mark.

The week slipped by. The crowds weren't great, but we did OK. To be sure, Connie, Cindy and Roxy showed up, and that made it more bearable. Bob and I were sort of counting the days.

On Friday, during break, I called home about ten-thirty.

No answer.

That was strange. Anne hadn't mentioned any plans for the evening, and I told her I would call. Not that I kept tabs on her, but we usually told each other if there was something going on, in case one needed to make contact. She certainly knew where I would be.

I called over the next two breaks.

No answer.

I was upset. Something was bugging me and I had a bad feeling.

By the time I got home at one forty-five, Anne was asleep. The next morning, Saturday, I asked her about it.

"I was out with Arthur," she told me.

"Arthur?"

"He asked me. I hadn't seen him in a long time, since before we were married." Arthur was Anne's first serious love. They met in high school. Soon after, they had lived together.

"Did you go to bed with him?"

Really, I hated to demean myself and Anne by asking this question, but the way things had been going I had to jump dead in the middle of it.

"Yes."

"Oh man..."

"But, Cindy told me you had been to bed with her. It only seemed fair to me." She took a breath. "Besides, something's been missing, and I wanted to find out."

Cindy and Anne had been best friends for years. At one time, Anne had told me she wouldn't mind if Cindy and I were lovers. That should have been my clue then and there, but I thought things would work out. I wanted them to. We both did.

"Look," I said, "for some reason I was always attracted to Cindy. But, I never would have acted on it except that you didn't seem to be turned on to me after a while, and said you didn't care. It was sort of self-defense."

"Well, for me too. There were some things I had to find out."

"But damn. I never went out on you, never tried to pick up anybody while playing at a bar, even on the road. I turned down people." (Never mind Poplar Bluff...) I took a deep breath.

"I love you, but I couldn't take being nearly celibate."

"Well..."

"Well, you never did think of me as a lover, did you." This was not a question.

"No."

"So why did we get married?"

"I love you. You're a good person." She really felt this way.

"So why don't we make love?"

"I don't know. I guess you just don't turn me on." She had a point. We had lots of fun together but didn't exactly set each other on fire.

"Well, I love you, but I can't take this anymore."

"What do you want, a divorce?"

"Yes."

It was stunning. Neither of us had thought of divorce. But when she asked, it popped out of my mouth. I said it without thinking. It was as if, in a moment of crisis, another part of me had taken over, some actual part of the body, more primal and direct.

Somehow, we knew there was no going back.

I was still in a daze when I got to Genova's that night, earlier than usual. Barry and Debbie were sitting at a table, having a drink before the show. I sat down with them, and was glad the lights were low. My eyes were really red.

"Hi Barry, hi Deb."

The waitress came over. I ordered a double Black Jack on the rocks and a burrito. I sat silently until my drink arrived.

"Boy," I said to Barry and Debbie, "I guess that Anne and I are going to get divorced."

Barry and Debbie didn't know Anne and me that well as a couple. They had met her a few times, but we had never had the opportunity to actually socialize.

"Oh yeah?" asked Barry.

"What happened, Frank?" asked Debbie.

"It's hard to say now, but we decided it would be best for us. We didn't beat each other up or anything, but I think it's been coming for a while."

Playing that night was terrifically difficult. I was constantly on the verge of breaking down. But it would have been worse not to be working.

Luckily, while I was on stage during the show, the only light was the spotlight on Bobby. We were in the dark.

On any given night, depending, playing in the dark can be hard, trying to see what we were doing. But that night I was grateful for the dim lights. In the deep, deep blue of the spotlight while Bobby sang Suspicious Minds, I was looking down, purposely not looking out at the audience. My fingers kept slipping, losing their grip on the strings from tears raining down on my bass.

Monday we began our last week at Genova's. Anne and I were still going to Biloxi together, although more for a swan song than for reconciliation. I tried to refrain from burdening the rest of the crew with my troubles, and diverted myself by talking to more of the women in the audience.

Crowds were thinning out at Genova's by the middle of the week.

We were lucky to have ten people in the place by closing. This was depressing, but we coasted as best we could.

Bobby had picked a candidate for my replacement on bass. A guy named Joe. He'd been coming to the show to get an idea of the workings, and by Thursday was ready to try out a few tunes. During our last break, Bob came up to me.

"Say, during this last set, how about if Joe sits in for a few tunes?"

"I don't mind," I said. "Be a nice interlude. Does he have a bass, or does he need mine?"

"He'll have to use yours."

I squinted at Bob. "He hasn't been eating ribs, has he?" I have this preternatural aversion to grease on my bass strings.

"No," he said, laughing.

We decided that Joe would play in the middle of the set. One of his tunes would be Brown Sugar by the Rolling Stones.

Come time, Bob called Joe up to play. I handed him my bass and went to step off stage. Bobby was sitting in the audience at a table, watching to see how Joe did.

Then I had an idea.

"Hey Bob, since I sing Brown Sugar, give me a mike and let me go down on the floor."

"Yeah!" his eyes flashed. "Joe doesn't sing. Do it!"

I got down on the dance floor, same as where Bobby did his act, and sang and performed while the band played. Hollywood even ran the spotlight. After the song, the band spontaneously went into the reprise that we always played after Bobby's show.

I pranced around, bowing. I wasn't mocking Bobby, just having fun. I wanted to see what it felt like up front.

Then I knelt to give "the blessing," as Bobby always did: Down on one knee, arms raised straight and high. Fingers in a "V," flip hands down at wrist to point at audience, so they applaud themselves.

Anyway, I did the blessing, and the music suddenly stopped.

I turned around to see Bob on the stage floor holding his sides, laughing, while Charles slumped over his drums, incapacitated. Barry was hiding his face in his hands. Poor Joe didn't know what to do.

Pete and Joe Genova loved it. The few customers still there also loved it. They applauded wildly, laughing.

Bobby was the only person who didn't look entirely pleased, but even he had to laugh, if only to keep up a front. The next day, Barry told me how later on that night, Bobby had asked him, "What's that guy on?" "I just laughed," Barry said.

"That was great," said Joe Genova. "When you gonna do the 'Frankie Stone Show' again?"

It was a hit. They made me do it again the next night.

Saturday night it was all over. We played a good show to a good crowd.

Bob and I packed our stuff. As for the rest of the Love Machine, they had at least another week to go at the Chestnut Inn, and nobody knew after that.

Ed paid us, and wished us good luck. He knew we wouldn't stay.

Lee tried to harass Bob for denting his truck door in Poplar Bluff.

"Y-you owe me a hundred d-d-dollars for that door, Bob." He tried to sound tough.

"I got about as much intention of paying you for it as you do of fixing it," said Bob. Then he turned and left.

Everyone was sad to see us go.

The fans.

Pete and Joe.

Especially Charles and Barry.

But, Bob had burnt out on the band business.

As for me, my whole life was turning inside out. A weird show, a broken marriage – what more could I ask?

Besides, I was going back to school. That much was certain, and I wanted to stay in town. But Bobby was still hell-bent about going on the road. I might have stayed, but for that. I could have used the work.

Five of us – Charles, Barry, Bob, Hollywood and Frankie Stone – walked out to the parking lot. It was July 22, 1978. The stars shone on a hot and humid Kansas City night.

We all shook hands and looked each other square in the eyes.

Bob and I got in our cars and drove off in different directions.

As I hit the freeway, I took a deep breath.

www.ingramcontent.com/pod-product-compliance
Lightning Source LLC
Chambersburg PA
CBHW070423010526
44118CB00014B/1882